Morning Mist

Stories from the Water's Edge

Barbie Loflin

WordCrafts

Morning Mist
Stories from the Water's Edge
Copyright © 2014
Barbie Loflin

Cover photography & design by David Warren

All rights reserved. No part of this book may be reproduced, stored in a retrieval system, or transmitted in any form or by any means – electronic, mechanical, photocopy, recording, or otherwise – without the prior written permission of the publisher. The only exception is brief quotations for review purposes.

Unless otherwise noted, Scripture quotations are from THE HOLY BIBLE, NEW INTERNATIONAL VERSION®, NIV® Copyright © 1973, 1978, 1984, 2011 by Biblica, Inc.® Used by permission. All rights reserved worldwide.

Scripture quotations marked "Message" are from the Message Bible *The Message* by Eugene H. Peterson, copyright© 1993, 1994, 1995, 1996, 2000, 2001, 2002. Used by permission of Tyndale House Publishers, Inc.

Scripture quotations marked "KJV" are from The Holy Bible, King James Version, public domain.

Scripture quotations marked "NCV" are from the New Century Version. Copyright © 1987, 1988, 1991 by Thomas Nelson, Inc. Used by permission. All rights reserved.

Exerpt from "The Velveteen Rabbit, or how toys become Real" by Marjery Williams, public domain.

Published by WordCrafts Press
Tullahoma, TN 37388
www.wordcrafts.net

OTHER BOOKS BY BARBIE LOFLIN

I Wish Someone Had Told Me
(Ten week In-Depth Bible Study)
© 2002 *Poured Out Ministries*

Poured Out
From a Place of Deep Waters
(Poetry and Short Stories)
©2003 *Poured Out Ministries*

Suddenly Sunday
(12 Week Devotional Journal)
©2005 *Poured Out Ministries*

Positioned for Transition
(Arrows in His Hand)
©2008 *Poured out Ministries*

Thank you, Sandi Accousti –
My editor extraordinaire.
Your joy, your gift, your heart –
Bless and amaze me.
You continue to make me believe
I can actually write like John Boy.

FOREWARD

I have four sisters. I am the one in the middle. To my knowledge, I was the only one who ever went fishing with my dad. Of course, my going had nothing to do with my skill or expertise; it was based purely on my desire to be with him. Simple. I still remember standing on that lakeshore with my toes digging into the mud, the cool morning mist kissing my face and making my unruly hair even curlier. I remember thinking how blessed people must be who live near the water and can frolic in the mist every morning. And just imagine, they could stick their toes in lake mud anytime they wanted.

I cannot remember another time in my ten

years with him, that we were actually all alone together. I remember lying awake the night before wondering how many huge fish I was going to catch and thinking how proud he was going to be when he saw what a fine fisherman I was. But as I stood there that morning by my dad, casting and re-casting, reeling and re-reeling, baiting the hook time after time, it became apparent; *my dream of becoming a famous bass fisherman and traveling the world with my dad in a Winnebago with a fancy boat trailing behind just wasn't going to come true.*

So I stood there on the bank praying *Just one fish, God... is that too much to ask? One lousy fish. But, it was not to be so. Not even one...*

Still, much to my chagrin, the stringer was absolutely loaded with fish when we headed home later that morning. Daddy was happy and I was mortified. What a loser!

As we walked up the broken sidewalk to our little country home, my mother came out the screen door and asked how it had gone. I waited for the embarrassment that I knew was coming. *Oh, I caught forty million, but Barbie was dead weight. She was the albatross around my neck...(I have always been a little dramatic).*

Of course my father would never have actually said something like that, but I was just so disappointed in myself.

But what my dad did at that moment just blew me out of the water. When my mom asked how it had gone, he proudly took the stringer out of the cooler and held it high, fish hanging off every hook, and then he did something I found quite stunningly beautiful; he handed the opposite end of the stringer to me, allowing me to hold it out right alongside him – as if I'd had some grand part in their catching. Only then did he answer my mother's question, with a wink at me, and a "Well, we did pretty good."

We...he said we.

I remember thinking, *but I didn't do anything! He did all the work, and caught all of the fish.* Yet, he stood right there and let me share in his victory, made me look good when I had no true right to.

As a little girl, I thought about that for a long time. And then I finally came to the only conclusion that made sense. My dad had let me shine simply because he loved me and because he knew I loved him; loved him enough to want to be out there by the water with him before the sun had come up. It mattered to him that I had gotten up sleepy-headed and packed a couple of little sandwiches. It meant something to him that I just wanted to be there for one reason alone - because he was there.

And you see, what I got from that encounter was far more than I could have imagined. For you see, he was not looking for someone who could throw a line. He could have called one of his friends if he needed help catching those fish. What he had wanted was time with me. Me – the barefoot, tomboy, curly headed, missing front teeth, June-bug catching, creek-wading, dress-hating, misfit middle child. He simply liked my company. Go figure.

And in those moments, I had my daddy all to myself. I was a part of what he was doing. He laughed with me. He talked to me like I was something special, and when all was said and done, he let me share in the fruit of His labor. One wink told me we were a team and everybody else would have to run to catch up to what we had. That wink formed an impenetrable circle around a father and daughter and said to all comers, "You ain't part of this club." And in this girl's overactive imagination, we were now and forever the *sootsotwadatwe*- The *Secret Order of the Society of Those Who Always Dwell at the Water's Edge*.

Ah, childhood.

Me, my father, and the water in the cool of the morning… probably the most precious memory I have of my dad, the grand Pooh-Bah of the Sootsotwadatwe's.

Forty years later, the parties have changed a bit, but walking in the mist remains a morning ritual for me. Me, my (heavenly) Father, and the Water Word in the wetness of a new days dawning.

I rise early. He meets me there. Together we sweep away to the water's edge. I have Him all to myself. The world is barely waking, and I am headed straight into a secret adventure. He is there. He talks to me, we laugh together, and He makes me feel like there is nowhere else He would rather be. And do you know what? When we come away from the waters, though it is He who has done the work, He always hands me my side of the stringer - a word, a poem, a short story, a vignette – a memento of our time together, and allows me to hold it out as if I had something to do with it…though we both know better.

And it is these mementos, sweet and personal God-moments – moments when He revealed His heart to me, teaching me as only a Father can teach His child – along with poignant spiritual revelations, and deep awakenings that pierced my heart and made me shake my head in wonder, these are the offerings you hold in your hand.

You will also find a couple of stories which were previously published in my earlier offering, *Suddenly Sunday*. I felt compelled to revisit and include them in this compilation because they truly are stories from the water's edge.

I pray you are touched. I pray you are blessed, and I pray that you leave longing to write your own pages, because, beloved, we all have a story to tell. Our lives are literally filled with learning opportunities drenched in profound intimacy with the God of the Universe.

One of my favorite prayers comes from *Isaiah 50:4 He wakens me morning by morning, wakens my ear to listen like one being taught.*

So I pray, Father, awaken our hearts this morning to be taught of You. Take us through what can sometimes seem a world of mist, to the centering clarity of Your gracious and divine will.

May we always be awake enough to be a part of what You are doing.

The day is beautiful
The morning crisp
Your toes are ready
The Father waits
It is time to go
Into the Mist

WILLOW

When I was a little girl we had a huge weeping willow tree in the front yard of our house. It sat to the right of the porch and encompassed the whole area. I remember feeling so small beneath its branches. I would crawl under the canopy and hide behind the fragrant green curtain, and there, in the depths of this captivatingly lush beauty I would build my kingdom… for I had been given a Burger King crown made of shiny paper and that most assuredly made me royalty.

I found that old metal serving spoons made wonderful scepters and came in quite handy as shovels, most capable of digging moat trenches around sturdy trunk roots, and Dixie cups can fill that ravine quite readily after many trips to mama's kitchen. I discovered that small plastic dishes look most appetizing laden with big old acorns harvested from the oak nearby, and that crazy squirrels are not afraid to come and retrieve their stolen bounty from little red headed girls who scream and run at the sight of them.

In my kingdom I found that stray dogs love lonely laps, and that mothers yell really loud when they find nothing but your legs sticking out from under the neighbor's collie. And did you know that if you lay on the ground with your hands behind your head and squint just a bit, sunshine through willow branches looks just like heaven exploding all around you? Dust mites floating on effervescent rays become mini-Glenda's passing through on their way home to Oz and tree frogs become sentinels calling forth into neighboring reptilian lands.

It was pure magic. There was nothing like it upstairs in my bedroom or in any other place I had ever been. Huge, vast, limitless and intimate, it was all mine. And it was right there in my front yard all along. I can remember thinking, how long has this been here and why didn't anyone tell me? And then I remember this special kind of excitement just knowing that it was all right there at my fingertips. All I had to do was come out of my safe little room and take a few steps, reach out my hand and sweep aside the branches, and step behind the curtain.

And the kingdom waited.

(Let those who have an ear, hear...)

Seems like forever ago, but I still feel the sense of drawing. Just the thought of the lazy willow blowing in the breeze makes me long for home, spoons, drooling dogs and tin foil crowns.

Oh, but dear ones, I have found a more wonderful kingdom. With one sweep of the heart I found myself behind its curtain. And like the first, I found myself asking, how long has this been here and why didn't anyone tell me? For in this kingdom, there dwells a true, honest-to-goodness King. And He is good and kind and powerful. Beautiful to behold and easy to serve.

The King Who rules this Kingdom carves mountain ranges with a breath and fills oceans with words. His voice sounds like many waters and His heart pounds melodies. He can speak floods and paint rainbows, heal wounds and scatter stars across night skies. He walks with the pauper and feeds the hungry, covers the naked and comforts the mourning. Yet He is enthroned in majesty, surrounded by praise and exalted by The Elders. High and lifted up, yet touchable and accessible.

In His Kingdom, less is more and the first is last. In His Kingdom rulers serve and servants rule, and in His Kingdom, filthy rags are made righteous - scarlet sins become snow white. In His Kingdom lions lay down beside lambs and there is a tree whose branches truly do provide healing for all of the nations…

It must be a willow.

Your kingdom is an everlasting kingdom,
and your dominion endures through all generations.
The LORD is faithful to all his promises
and loving toward all he has made.
Psalm145:13

TURNING STONES

There is a time for everything, and a season for every activity under heaven...a time to scatter stones and a time to gather them...
Ecclesiastes 3:5

There is something to be said of turning stones.

When I was an eight year old tomboy living on a dusty old road called Walls Hollow, one of my most wonder-filled pastimes was perusing gravel. (Yes, I am easily entertained). Gray rock, mundane and nondescript, possessed a lure I found somehow irresistible. Though the grown-up eye might find it common, I knew that lurking just beneath the surface of the ordinary was the potential for the extraordinary.

I knew that if you turned the stone and looked at it from all angles, you might find a pink or white quartz-like composite lying in wait for those who still had a heart that sought beauty – even in dirt.

I had happened upon that supreme knowledge much by accident, but it was an encounter that marked me… *Pink Diamonds!* What I had seen as plain old stone before, in that moment of revelatory beauty, had now become potential treasure, and it was mine, all mine! What I had once ignored I now became obsessed with. I could not walk on an ordinary gravel road without feeling a pull to look under the stones. I just had to see what was just beneath the surface, what lay on the other side. While others ran ahead, or left me altogether, I walked slowly, stooping to turn the gravel in my hand, abiding the dust cloud, knowing that at any time, the hidden beauty would miraculously appear.

In my days of innocent searching, subtle nuances drew my eye and held my attention. Was that a shard of pink? What is that running along the edge? Is that what I think it is? Fueled by faint knowledge and the draw of previous findings, I was hooked.

From side to side, I staggered along the potholed road, chasing glimmers, thoughts and perceptions. I knew it was there. I just had to look until I found it. I never once thought the trove barren. I just had to take another step, turn a couple more stones, not be moved by the others who told me there was nothing there.

Turn, turn, turn. Yes! There it was. I knew it! Pink quartz in ordinary gravel. Though some thought it without value, I knew it was the most amazing stuff. It was just beautiful to me and I knew that God had hidden it away just for me to find. Pure gifts...and those little treasures brought me such great joy. I simply could leave nothing behind. I would pick it up, take it home and wash it, and place it with my private collection...and oh what I collection I had. By the time the box was full, it was too heavy for me...so it rested in a secret place. The box stayed securely tucked under my bed, because I thought to leave them out in the open would be to advertise my wealth to others, and that seemed like bragging to me.

You see, I had stumbled onto a gold mine and could not believe my good fortune. Nor could I understand that others might be immune to its draw.

How could anyone walk past this beauty without stopping to gather some for themselves? One glimpse, one holding of the bounty in my hand, and I was captivated.

The stone paths were treasure fields to me.

Much the same has happened in my study of the Word. Though I in no way want to infer that the Word is a stony field, I have come to find that the words flowing upon the pages have become (to many) an ordinary and mundane thing. So often have they walked these pathways, they no longer take time to notice the stones, much less stop and turn them. They tread the obvious, and never take the time to hunger for the hidden. They love the beautiful jewels mined by others, but rarely consider their own propensity for digging. They have no tolerance for the dust that gets kicked up when searching on their own.

It took only one uncovering, one vein of true beauty to hook me. It was the simplest of moments. It was four words that released the rainbow of color, unleashed the hunger for the other side of the Word. Four words slowed me down and made me allow the others to run on ahead as I kicked up dust and got my hands in the dirt. Brilliant, incandescent and pure, the colors of eternity rose from the page and I grabbed the treasure that would fill my heart and send me on an unending, stone turning quest...four little words:

"In the beginning, God..."

And that, dear one, is what I call *Eternal Pink Diamonds*...

Ahhhhh.

CATS & BATHTUBS

One of my favorite childhood television shows was *The Waltons.* It was simple, honest and filled with kids like the ones I went to school with. However, my favorite part of the show was the last 90 seconds. Every evening John Boy would go to his room, sit down at the desk beneath his window, and begin to write about his day. I used to imagine that I would one day write eloquent words telling about my life, my adventures, my thoughts and my dreams. As I listened to the Walton family calling out their signature good nights, I would reach for my journal, pretending that I, like John Boy, was a real writer. Thursday nights. Eight O'clock, Me and John Boy.

Nothing fancy, just a simple dream, but a dream I have now come to see as a God-dream. How very dear the memory is to my heart. Now, many years later, I have come to realize that it was not merely a dream but an awakening and recognition of a deeper part of my spiritual identity. The eternity on my heart was whispering a love of words into my soul, and with every syllable the captivation became more complete. This was God rushing through a would-be writers veins.

You see He gave me dreams that lined up with His plan for my life. And more than likely, he has done the same with you. Your dreams may well be the prompting of the Holy Spirit toward your particular calling or gift. (I am pretty sure many first writing attempts were birthed while looking through John-Boys window. I gnawed through countless no. 2 pencils in my quest to choreograph that completely perfect word-dance.)

As a child, I could not begin to get my mind around a dream quite so big. Becoming a writer was equivalent to...oh I don't know...teaching a cat to run its own bath water and jump in. I simply could not dream that big. Just couldn't imagine it. Oh, but He could. This wonderful God could not only imagine it, but could bring it to pass. Now, five books and countless opportunities later, I have come to understand that God's plan is never limited by or to my abilities.

Amazing, huh?

I have truly come to see that my dream had very little to do with what I could do, and everything to do with His grace and goodness. In this, God is teaching me every day that the boundaries I have set for my life are not His boundaries.

I believe with all of my heart that He is calling all of us to take a leap of faith and begin to believe Him for the big stuff - the things we used to dream about that may seem totally out of reach. It is time to stop relying on what we have and rely on all that He possesses.

He's got some stuff!

So, dear ones, anyone out there got a John-Boy dream hidden away in the dusty confines of a long-locked hope chest? Get it out. Dust it off. Be brave enough to ask God about it...

Then grab the cat and head for the bathtub.

THE MUSIC BOX

On about my sixth birthday, my mother bought me a music box. It was your standard little white, flowery, square box that I presume most little girls had at one point or another in their childhood. When you opened the lid of the box a small spring-held ballerina would arise and begin her twirling dance. I loved that music box. For years I could hear the tune playing in the back of my soul.

What I could not get out of my mind was not the simple plinking away of the tiny notes, but instead, the sound of my mother's voice, as she would wind the tiny box and begin the tucking in process… *Around the world I searched for you…*sheets and blankets clean and crisp from hanging in the sunshine on our clothesline, now deftly drawn up to my chin; *I traveled on when hope was gone...* sides tucked in close, now safe and sound, the smell of ivory soap still clinging to her skin; *I knew somewhere, sometime, somehow...* hand upon my forehead, she'd push the unruly curls back and lean in and kiss me right between the eyes and smile... *You would look at me; I'd see you smile...* "I love you, Barbie..." She would turn, wind the box one more time, click off the light, and I would watch her chenille bathrobe clear the door frame as her house shoes patted down the hallway into the living room.

Though no longer in the room, still she remained; the touch, the aroma, the love, flowed through the song and dance of the ballerina and the toy tones of the inexpensive box. *Around the world I searched for you...* I was loved and comforted and completely enthralled.

That phrase always made me feel wonderful on the inside. So wonderful in fact that I would keep rewinding the music box until my mother would finally call out "Last time, dear." You see, I believed that my mother had chosen that music box specifically for me and this was her way of letting me know she had longed for me all of her life. In those moments I felt unbelievably special. I mean I must have been for her to say that she had searched the whole world for me.

Time after time in the lonely stillness of the night, I would slide the music box deep beneath my covers and wind the tiny key… releasing my mother's love into the dark recesses of the room, *Around the world I searched for you...* and I would close my eyes and rest.

Even today, the tune winds through my heart and tears halt just beneath the surface of this child-turned-woman's eyes. But now, in my advancing years, a deeper, more profound voice has been added to the song. There is now a peaceful tucking that has nothing to do with blankets but everything to do with linen cloths. A leaning in and rustling that has nothing to do with unruly curls, but everything to do with a rebellious nature. A kiss that still hits between the eyes and goes straight to the heart.

In inky blackness and starry night He sings

over me. Always about His ministrations He hovers and covers and sees to my well being, His goodness and His constant song reminding me that I am His and He absolutely did search the whole world for me.

And in this moment, the song continues...
I feel unbelievably special...
And sought.

LET GO

Sometimes the most frustrating thing in the world can be trying to forget the past. We remember old wounds and unkind words quite easily. It is as if with each replaying of the incident, it becomes etched a bit deeper upon our soul. We hit the rewind button, listen to the whispers of the enemy and fall into the pit of self-pity, crying all the while in our best I-don't-deserve-this martyrs' voice, "Why do you not take this from me, Lord? Why must I suffer so with these memories?" *(Anguish best portrayed with back of the hand to the forehead, slight hesitance between words and lips trembling as the voice falters and breaks...)*

Ever been there? A wound that should have

healed forever ago continues to cause you pain because you continue to expose it and invite infection through constant picking. Selah. (Pause calmly and think upon these things).

As a child I was forever falling out of trees, off of swings, into ditches, off of bicycles. To say I was not the most feminine flower in the garden would be a vast understatement. I had a lot of fun giving my mom all of that grey hair. During all of these "adventures" there were inevitable scrapes, cuts and bruises. I would hobble into the kitchen ('cause that's where you found my mother at any hour of the day), my hands clenched over the offended area, the first words from my mother's mouth were always, "Come here, honey. Let me see what has happened." Whiny, irritable, but a bit pleased by the attention, I slowly and dramatically submitted to her instructions.

Inevitably, she would lift me onto the counter and with greatly feigned anguish I would allow her to open my grimy fingers to reveal the wound. (Imagine the grimace of a freckled, two front teeth missing, sun burned nose kind of mischief face). Her next words were always, "Oh, see, that's not so bad." I use to think; *Funny how things are 'not that bad' when it isn't your own pain you are dealing with. Easy to say that when **your** life is not flashing in front of your eyes...*but I digress.

Anyway, she would take a soft washcloth, run it under warm water and gently cleanse the area. (She knew if she grabbed the Bactine squeeze bottle she would not see me for days). She would then hold the warm cloth against the wound until it started to feel better (and the gravel fell out). *What a miracle a mother's touch is!* Her final act would be to apply a healing balm (AKA Vaseline - that magical potion that heals all, gets your head unstuck from between the porch railing and makes your hair stay in place while soothing your chapped lips at the same time) and seal the wound with a bandage to keep out infection.

Her instructions were to leave the bandage on and not to keep opening and closing it - because that is most definitely our tendency when it comes to wounds; we want to show everyone and remind ourselves how bad it really was. I find that we have this morbid sense of inclusion when it comes to battle scars. Still, I knew the only time that bandage was to be removed was when *mama said so.* After all, everyone knows if *"You keep opening that bandage up and looking at it and it's gonna get infected."*

I also think she just knew somehow that I would need her there when I had to take another look. She knew I would not be able to keep my own hands off of it and I would need her comfort if there were another cleansing to take place.

I do not have to tell you where I'm going with this. Dear heart, the first step in any healing process is taking our hands off of the wound and letting the Father take a good look. Only in His presence can we see things without fear ruling and pain overtaking us. With and in Him the cleansing, the assurance, and the comfort can begin.

Yes, my friend, outside of our clenched fists there is healing. All we have to do is...

Let go.

FOCUS

At the age of fifteen, I had my first real date. I remember it distinctly. I was living with my grandmother at the time and thought my ship had finally come in. I was going on an honest to goodness, guy-pick-you-up-in-a-car, date.

It wasn't that I had actually liked the boy that much when he asked me out; it was everything that had happened since the asking. I had begun to FOCUS. What would I wear? How would I do my hair? How clean could I get granny's house before he walked in it to pick me up? What would he wear? Where would we go? What would we do? Was he THE ONE? Would he like me? What if I bit into the pizza and it was too hot and I pulled burning cheese out of my mouth in front of him?

What does one wear to the emergency room when burned by pizza cheese?

By the time Saturday morning arrived, I was a wreck. I think I was dressed, hair done and in full make-up by 7:00 … AM. All I had left to do for the next twelve hours was lay in front of my granny's old turntable and listen to Boston's "More Than a Feeling."

Needless to say, by the time he arrived in his black T-Top Trans Am, I already knew how many children we would have, (two - Brandy and Chayse – with "special" spelling), what kind of house we would live in, (two story red brick with a veranda), what color my Camaro would be, (candy-apple red), and that our black Persian cat would be named Fifi.

Poor guy, he thought we were going out for a coke.

So, what happened during those twelve hours that took me from getting a coke with a boy, to spending the rest of my days on earth with him? Focus.

For as he thinketh in his heart, so is he.
Proverbs 23:7 7 (KJV)

We truly do fall in love with those things that capture our thoughts and hold our focus. When we invest our attentions our heart soon follows. So, I suppose the question of the week must become, "*What am I thinking about all of the time?*"

What, or who occupies *your* mind? Where is your treasure? For it is there that you will find your heart.

I do not think I ever went out with that guy again... but thanks to a healthy imagination and a whole lot of intense focus, for twelve hours in a fifteen-year-old girl's life, I was married with children.

Wow!

Can you say focus?

ENOUGH

I grew up in Walls Hollow, a small coal mining community in East Tennessee. The curvy dirt road was easy to miss if you were not looking for it. A meandering dance of memorized potholes led into the woods where small plots of land had been cleared by those strong and determined enough to wield an ax and hold tight to a tiller. I remember well the days we would carry a sack lunch and sit out on the ground while Daddy, Papaw and my uncles worked our few acres, making a place for our house to be built. No bulldozers touched the soil, only worn leather work boots and buckets of sweat.

It was on our first visit to the hollow that Bum

adopted us. He had sorrowful brown eyes and coarse red/brown hair. He was gangly and uncoordinated and his ribs showed plainly against his taught skin. His back left leg had obviously been broken when he was small and had healed into a now useless appendage. He was starving, pitiful, and broken…and as he grabbed the bologna sandwich out of my hand, I thought he was the most beautiful hound dog in the whole world. I decided right then and there that he would be mine…'cause he needed me.

I did not call him Bum; my daddy did. He would watch Bum skulking around begging and tell us to run the "bum" off. Eventually Daddy would fall in love with the sad soul, but his name, Bum, would stick. Bum was my constant companion in those years. He ran the hills with me, waded the creeks, sat patiently at the bottom of trees as I climbed high and sat in their branches. Bum would run beside me as I rode my bike down dusty trails, often becoming entangled in the wheels in his desire to be close, sending us both tumbling. He would shake himself, jowls flapping, and then look at me as if to ask, *Why did you run over me?* Still, he would happily keep pace as we started back on our journey.

I loved that dog for several reasons, but the biggest reason was that he openly adored me. I could tell when he looked at me that I was enough. He was not daydreaming about other children in other fields. He was not thinking, *what is up with her hair?* No. Bum loved me. By the same token, I never thought… *wish he wasn't crippled or could run faster.*

He was enough.

Beautifully, completely, enough.

Love makes us enough.

In a world where it is easy to fall short, it is a wonderful thing to know that you are enough.

Many of us walk through our Christian lives feeling like God has His mind on someone else. We think if we could just be better, or funnier, or smarter, or more talented… or less crippled, He would love us more. But you know what? His love makes us enough.

Who could ask for more?

Morning Mist

> *Why is everyone hungry for more?*
> *"More, more," they say. "More, more."*
> *I have God's more-than-enough.*
> *Psalm 4:5-7 (Message)*

WATER TO ME

I have never been the type to wade gently into the water looking all graceful and dignified. I am more the *run-jump-hold-your-nose-plunge-splash* kind of girl. I always thought the others looked pretty, but knew they could not possibly be having nearly as much fun as I was. After all, while they were standing ankle deep in tepid salt water, the waves splashing gently around their ankles, I was soaked, sputtering, coughing like crazy, and had seaweed in my teeth... Ah, the bliss.

Your eyes stung, every scrape (and I had plenty) came alive with the fire of painful cleansing, and your feet sank into things best left undiscovered.

My sisters all thought I was nuts (not much has changed, by the way). They were girl-girls. They had no idea how much fun a starfish could be when stuck to your leg, or how it felt to be thrown from a horse or hit in the face with a basketball. My sisters did not know the thrill of stealing third base, or riding dirt bikes without mom's permission. They did not know that stars are best viewed at 1:00 am after climbing out your window and onto the roof in your orange converse high-tops and nightgown.

Simple things, really. They could have done any of these things... but no... they liked it safe and organized and all planned out. I began most mornings looking for socks and homework, while my sisters rolled their eyes and tapped their dainty toes in frustration.

I remember running out the front door one morning, jumping down the front steps and falling very ungracefully at the feet of my embarrassed older sisters. They looked at my mom and asked, "Oh, mother, what are we going to do about Barbie?"

Duh, Hello! I thought. *You could help me get up!*

You see, I thought they were asking what they should do at the moment, when in fact it was my whole life that left them scratching their heads and walking many paces ahead of me in public.

I did not fit in. I never have. I have always heard a different drum beat in my spirit. I knew that life was supposed to be a grand adventure, and I did not want to miss a moment of it indoors where the world lost its wondrous beauty. I needed sunshine on my face and cool grass beneath my bare feet. I needed hills to climb and puppies to wrestle. I loved to laugh and I loved to sing at the top of my voice… with only God listening.

I learned at an early age that God created creeks for lonely children with curly red hair, and that dogwood blooms fit perfectly in small hands with dirty fingernails. For, you see, God has always loved me more than I deserved and more extravagantly than I could fathom.

He has always been water to me.

A SIMPLE LIFE

I loved going to the ocean when I was a child.

We did not have any money to speak of, but every year we would make the trek to Daytona Beach for a full week. It has been 28 years since we took such a trip, but I remember it like it was yesterday.

Mom would put us all to bed about 10:00 PM so we would be nice and tired. She would let us sleep until about 2:00 AM when we would smell the chicken frying in the kitchen. Mama always fried up some chicken for the drive. It took a lot of money to feed four girls and two parents, so we ate in the car along the way. We knew if the chicken was frying it was time to get ready. We didn't get up, mind you.

We didn't do that 'til it was time to go. But in my mind's eye, I was already walking the gritty sand beach feeling the sun on my freckled cheeks.

We would all pile into the black station wagon at around 3:00 AM, still in our pajamas; sleep still our closest companion, and the smell of warm chicken and the sound of Mama and Daddy's muted voices would put us back to sleep. We'd awaken around 7:00 or 8:00 and the "are we there yet's" would begin in earnest.

I did not know as a child that others had more than I did, or perhaps that I was even looked down upon because of my family's poverty. I had no idea that my shoes were not supposed to be too big, or that all moms' did not make their children's clothes. I did not know that all trips to Florida did not end at the Thunderbird Hotel, or that the drive could be made in air-conditioned vehicles with stops at actual restaurants... and it was beyond my comprehension that my mama's fried chicken was not the food of kings.

Today I know the blessing of air-conditioned

cars and wearing shoes that I have chosen. I know the feel of store-bought clothes upon my skin and the luxury of restaurants on long drives.

Yes, God has been extravagant in His provision for my family over the years. Still, in all of the change there has been a constant…My mama's fried chicken is still the food of Kings.

The years of financial lack were nothing in comparison to the great wealth we enjoyed in that station wagon my daddy spray-painted black. We would sing so loud the cars passing us would turn and stare…*of course it could have been the spray paint*, but we thought it was because of the beautiful music coming from within. We would laugh so hard we cried. Mama would pass out chicken and paper cups full of cold water. The wind blew through the windows and ruffled our handmade clothes, and my daddy would laugh a rich, throaty laugh as the passing drivers shook their heads in dismay.

And in those moments, the world was rich and wet and wonderful…and we were fully invested.

Sometimes we have it all right in front of us,

but cannot see what we have for all that we think we want. What strange and greedy creatures we have turned out to be.

> *A simple life in the Fear-of-GOD*
> *is better than a rich life with a ton of headaches.*
> *Proverbs 15:16 (Message)*

THE WEDDING

I stood and looked out over the field in front of my mother's house. Acres of old garden and dried hay stretched before me. The Blallock's old farmhouse stood on the hill across the dirt road, a stark white contrast to the deepening shadows of the day. In between the two aged dwellings something wonderful was taking place – something of eternal significance; my cousin was marrying his bride.

I watched as men in overalls and women in gingham dresses made their sojourn across the field, not to an arbor, or a lace covered gazebo, but simply to the center of the field... the same field that had grown their crops, fed their families, and resounded with the feet of running children.

The tender circle began to form.

There was no wedding coordinator to lead the way, or ushers to seat grand ladies, there was simply a gathering – a gathering of good people.

As the country minister made his way to the center of the circle, the father of the groom threw a stone at a barking hound dog, prompting it to head back to its lazy perch upon the worn rug that graced the weathered front porch. Then I saw them – the bride and the groom – walking hand in hand toward the gathering. She wore a simple white dress, and he – well, he shone brightly in his dress uniform – the same he would wear when he left for Iraq the same week.

As the couple walked close, the circle opened to receive them, then closed once again around them. They were surrounded by generations of faithful hearts and strong backs, generous souls with calloused hands. And as I watched, the good people bowed to thank their Creator for the blessed bounty of this day. A day without crystal goblets and chandeliers. A day without string quartets and satin slippers. A day when cotton dresses and work boots would stand witness to God's goodness in fields of promise.

The sun began its descent just as the preacher whispered shyly to the groom – "You can kiss her now." The soldier bent his head and kissed his pink-cheeked bride, holding her close to his heart, as the circle grew quite small. Hands were shaken, backs patted and embraces shared as the couple was absorbed into the hearts of their kin.

Men and women, hand in hand, turned and made their way across the field and down the road to their own dwellings.

The sun hid its face behind the night…and the field brought forth life, once again.

AND THEY DANCED

I went to my daughter's school some time ago to have lunch with her. As I sat in the hallway waiting for her class to appear, I watched the children make their way through the cavernous hallways.

Single file. Mouths shut tightly. The familiar clip, clip of the teacher's heels pounding on the tiled floors. As they filed past I began to hum…(imagine a British accent) *all in all it's just another brick in the wall.* Oops…where did that come from? Pink Floyd? Hello!

When the next class came up the hallway, I watched as they marched silently, single file, close enough to the wall the keep the corridor clear. Hands clutching little metal lunch boxes, I began to sing…O EEE oh, O EEE Oh…(Picture Wizard of Oz march…)

The third class started around the corner, hands by their sides, stepping in unison, silence and order reigned…until I saw him. Yes, you could not miss him. As he rounded the corner the single file line took a detour. Arms flailing, hips moving to some unknown beat, the little boy danced his way down the corridor, everyone around him acting as if he did not exist.

As he danced, I sang, "Celebrate good times. Come on…it's a celebration…" (Yes, still a child of the 70's) I made it to the second "celebrate" before our mental music came to a screeching halt.

Then came the voice. You know the voice. It is that accusatory, disappointed, belittling voice that has told you all of your life that you must conform and fit in – the voice that sucks the life out of laughter, steals candy from children and pops bright and beautiful balloons mid-flight. The I've-been-living-on-this-planet-so-long-all-of-my-dreams-have-died-so-yours-must-die-too, voice. From somewhere down the hall, just around the corner, I hear its weight shifting from burdened grown up, to carefree boy. *The voice* bellows, "That will be just about enough out of you, mister! You will now have a SILENT LUNCH! (Picture the special effect echo)…silent lunch…silent lunch…

A hush fell. Accusing eyes darted toward the child who had dared break the rule. Dancing! And in the middle of a school no less! How dare he?!

At the sound of the voice the dancing stopped. The little boy stepped obediently into line, following the same path as everyone else, and went into the cafeteria, where he would now partake of his SILENT LUNCH. Order was restored once again. Chaos ceased to reign. All was well. The joyous dancing had been brought under control.

Mission accomplished, *Voice*.

Guys, let me tell you something, if I could go back and do it over, I would dance down every single hallway and risk the silent lunch.

I felt the little dancer dude's pain. I thought about the many (and I do mean many) times Mrs. Margaret Bunch would sneak up behind me during naptime and swat my backside with that paddle just because I had something very life-changing and urgent to tell the person asleep on the mat next to mine. I mean, had it not been for this strong gifting of conversation that God has given me, (smile) I might have been truly damaged!

There will be many times in your life – if you love God with all of your heart – that you will absolutely feel compelled to a dance to a supernatural heart rhythm, a different drum. You will hear music that no one else hears, feel a lightness in your step that woos you to tango instead of march. And when you feel His music, Darlin', dance.

Be willing to risk a silent lunch or two. Be ready to release what people think about you in exchange for caring what He thinks. If you never risk it, you will miss the transcendent *Celebrate* moments.

Dear one, never let clicking heels, wagging tongues, or *The Voice* stop your dance. Life is too short.

Or, as my four-year-old daughter so aptly sang as she danced her way absently down the aisle at church… "Our God is an awesome God…

so *shake, shake, shake, - shake, shake, shake, shake your booty."*

Selah.

PERSPECTIVE

I had a conversation with a friend this past week. She was talking about how every time she started to dig into the Word and started getting closer to the Lord, something bad happened. It seemed as if she believed that her pursuit of God was bringing about these attacks. It made her want to stop in her tracks. After all, if things were just going to get worse, she should back off.

    I looked at her and said, "I believe you've got it all backwards. You are not looking at this in the right way. You see I believe God knew the attacks were coming, so He drew you into the Word and initiated the time of deeper intimacy. He wanted you full and grounded when all of this hit. Just think of where you would be if your legs were not under you when all of this came down." She relaxed and you could see an appreciation for God's grace washing through her. This God she loves had prepared her for an onslaught.

Modern theology might ask, *"Well, why didn't He just stop the onslaught?"* But Biblical truth tells us *in the world **we will** have tribulation, but that we will overcome because He overcame.*

In God's mercy, He prepares us for times of tribulation if we will allow Him to do so. In His mercy, He had placed my friend in the protective covering of His presence before the storm came through. The enemy wanted her to think the storm came because of her proximity to God, when in truth it was her orbiting of God that saved her during the onslaught that had already been set in motion. What a marvelous God! How deeply He loves His children.

When my friend grabbed hold of this truth, you could see the peace and gratitude wash through her. Her faith was strengthened by a simple (but profound) change in perspective.

Another friend made an offhand remark,

"Why is it that every time I get ahead financially something happens? Everything I have saved is gone." I said, "How good of God to provide what you needed before you ever needed it. Now you do not have to go into debt to pay for this unexpected situation." They rolled their eyes, looked at me and said, "You are one of those glass-half-full people, aren't you?" They meant it as an indictment. I took it as a compliment. But you see, to me, the glass being even half full is just a blessing from God. There are many that have no water in the glass whatsoever.

I am blessed. I serve a good God who takes care of me. I choose to live my life magnifying the good and minimizing the bad. I will not spend my precious time on this planet mourning over what I think I do not have, but in gratitude over all that I have been given.

How will you choose to live?

Dear struggling soul, there is so much peace to be found in a simple changing of perspective.

Now, how about a glass of water?

THE NIGHT OCEAN

Last night I dreamed I could hear the sound of water breaking against a very close shoreline. It sounded like there was an ocean just outside my door.

A night-ocean.

The sound drew me; drew me on a very deep level.

In my dream I moved across the room and to the door and stepped out onto a balcony. It was high balcony and it overlooked the waters, and though it was dark as pitch, I knew from the sound that if the moon were to come out in full I would find myself literally suspended over the water...the sound was that close and that rich.

Rolling, undulating, crashing, breaking,

pounding upon the banks.

I wanted terribly to see what I knew was there, but it was too dark and there was no light to reflect off of the white crests. I ached with the longing of hearing but not seeing. I could not see...but I knew, and I leaned deep into the space in hope of catching just a glimpse of the sound.

Oh, that sound!

It washed through me. In my longing I cried, "Lord, I want to see the waters." He answered my heart, "Until you *see* the waters, let the sound sustain you. Trust in what you cannot see." And with His words, my heart pressed deeper and my spirit engaged the sound of many waters. I cried...and I longed...and I hoped. Wide awake, quickened, and humbled, I moved toward the waiting.

As I stood on this balcony the Lord reminded me that this is how we are to live this life He has given us. Trusting in what we cannot see, we cry out to Him in all that we do. We hear a sound in the spirit and we long for Him in the depths.

We quicken, because our hearts have heard

the waters, the sound of promise washing through us and pouring across eternity.

We hope, because our spirits resound with the rhythm of the waves.

We long, because we have tasted.

We yearn, because only He can satisfy.

We break, because His beauty unhinges all that held us together.

Yes, because of the breathtaking radiance of Christ we are fully and completely undone; marvelously melted. And we lean over earth's temporal balcony and listen with our hearts, for that for which we long and that which resounds within our spirits.

So what do we do as we await the waters only our spirits can hear?

We move toward the sound. With everything on the inside of us we shift forward. We move in prayer, in reverence, in worship, in silence, in hope, in faith, in deep anticipation. We make a decision to move toward Him in ways that cost us something. We sacrifice praise from a new altar of brokenness. We put off the old wine skins and allow Him to make new ones. We sing, we dance, we rejoice, we cry, we kneel, we pray.

We lean.

And we listen in the depths to this wonderful God of the night-ocean.

ACT LIKE IT

Last night I sat in stunned silence as the woman across from me turned beet-red in anger. I am quite sure her blood pressure went through the roof as her eyes filled with rage, her mouth turned down in a snarl, teeth bared and her arm shot out in an attempt to slap the police officer who was trying to settle things down and bring a level of calm. Nothing like a high school basketball game to bring out the best in people. (I can see the nodding of heads of high school parents everywhere.)

I thought about that woman today. She was old enough to be my mother. Old enough to know better. I thought about how stressful her life must be in order for her to go over the edge like that in a public arena, over a little ball going through a hoop. I thought about how out of focus things must be in her world – how out of line her thinking must have become. I wondered what happened to her peace, and if she had ever had any. I wondered if the Sunday previous she had sat in a pew somewhere and made any attempt whatsoever to connect with her Creator, her source of peace. I briefly thought to myself, *I just wonder if she is a Christian?* And that thought shocked me a little. Made me stop and ponder for a moment. Because that was not a question I would have even considered a few years ago. Back then I thought I knew what a Christian looked like and I thought I knew how they behaved.

But now? Now. For better or for worse, (worse - in my opinion) it's getting really hard to spot behavioral Christianity. Unfortunately, our skewed perceptions of grace have wrongly licensed our lower lifestyles. We do not believe God expects anything better of us, so we expect nothing of ourselves. We have issued ourselves get out of jail free cards for every wrong behavior, and in the process, the image of Christ is all but disappearing from our walk before man. We think we are walking examples of His mercy, when in fact we are misrepresentations of truth. We are perpetrators of a great universal injustice – we applaud a blemished bride and attempt to offer her to a Holy Groom in the name of some idealized, unscriptural, unceasing mercy.

I know, it seems like a heavy thing to derive from a mad woman at a basketball game – but where did our convictions go? When did the line between right and wrong disappear to be replaced by the gray ambivalence of cheapened grace? When did Christianity begin to wear the garments of watered-down morality and secular humanism? When did we stop paying attention to that still, small voice and start obeying this overfed, under-disciplined, highly sensitized flesh of ours?

As I look around, I miss the evidences of a life controlled by God. Not the thumped Bibles, or the bumper stickers. Not the bad comb-over's or three piece suits, the Aqua Velva, long skirts and pious faces; but the wise, gentle ways of a peace-filled existence. I miss the clean, simple, love-you-Jesus kind of hearts and lifestyles I must have dreamed about. I miss Christians who behave like they believe in the Holy and the Divine and the Sacred. I miss the deep appreciation for sins covered by precious blood that was shed through pain and sacrifice. And I miss the once-piercing awareness that a brutal price was paid for our redemption.

Say what you will, I still believe a life committed to Christ looks completely different than a life led by the senses. I still believe you can and should know a Christian when you look them in the eye...or watch their behavior. Tattoos, piercings, blue jeans, t-shirts, Dior or Durango, the love of Christ should radically and completely change us from the inside out. And I truly believe if the God you serve is not big enough on the inside to affect the behaviors on the outside, you may want to take a closer look at who you really are serving.

Dear ones, grace is not an enabler. It never has been and never will be.

It is a gift. We really should act like it.

So if you're serious about living this new resurrection life with Christ, act like it. Pursue the things over which Christ presides.

Colossians 3:1 (Message)

US AND WE

2010. Resolutions, promises, good intentions. You name it and it has been put out there into the atmosphere. When the ball dropped and the clock struck midnight renewed determinations filled the cosmos. *I am going to exercise. I am going to spend more time with family. I am going to pay my tithes. I am going to be nicer, be smarter, be happier, be richer, be thinner.* With whispered prayers and cries of exultation and revelry, crossed fingers, and fresh, clean diary page at the ready, we have stepped into a brand New Year of opportunity.

So, what are we going to do with this undeserved treasure we have been given?

You see, too many of our resolutions and revelations are singular in purpose and lonely in their course. We need some together time. We need some Body Life, family fun, generational blessings passed through the touch of a hand and the rubbing of a shoulder - the sharing of a conversation and a meal. We need impartation and corporate celebration. We need profound quiet in the midst of the community of many voices. We need to think bigger in our New Year meanderings. Let's think small globe (at the very least).

Guys, my prayer is that we would reach deep and bring "better" into the lives of everyone with whom God entrusts us to share this journey. I pray that those who have been forgotten, neglected, rejected, broken, bruised and abandoned would find their home in the hearts of His people. I pray that we will not repeat our sins, our failures, our transgression, and that our old habits will actually die... even if it is hard. I pray that lonely be abolished and separate be only for a time and by Spirit's unction. I pray that me time becomes us time, and all the Lone Rangers out there on the Jesus Frontier, finally find their Tonto's.

May this year be a year of fewer I's and more we's. May it be filled with less of mine and more of ours.

Can *we* just go there?

THERE IS ROOM
(Thoughts at Christmas)

Ahhhh. Home sweet home. Dust bunnies, dirty dishes, and a couple loads of laundry... FIVE GOLDEN RINGS... It is way too late, and way too close to Christmas for you to expect me to do anything coherent.

I just walked in from a wonderful Christmas program at church. I think pretty much all of you were there. (If not, you better start being faithful in your attendance... someone has taken your seat!) The house was full and the family was in rare form. What a wonderful exclamation point on an already joyous season.

As the orchestra struck the first strains and the choir began to swell, I snuggled into my seat, took a deep breath and relaxed for the first time in what seems like forever. I looked around the shadowed room and glimpsed the profiles of many that I hold dear (that would include you). I watched as babies crawled over weary mothers who continued to lift their voice in song. I watched sleeping infants drool on daddy's shoulders as rich baritone voices filled the air. I saw mothers and daughters sitting close together and fathers and sons nudging one another with elbows, as if to say, "This is pretty cool…in a manly way."

The sights and the sounds of Christmas surrounded me. Not the ones from the stage, though they were wondrous indeed, but the ones in the seats around me. What I heard was the laughter of heart's content and full, the camaraderie of strangers and friends that have slowly and perfectly, without notice, turned into family. In our midst there was a bustling quiet of peace restored and the unspoken gratitude of outcasts having finally found their place in this world.

Home-folk, doing what home-folk do: loving, extending, welcoming, accepting, nourishing, making room for one another. Singing a spacious and welcoming song of genuine embrace. A song that made me feel like I was sitting by the hearth with friends...

And this (I believe) is where the true sounds of Christmas can overtake you, just as they did me. For remember, two thousand years ago, in a crowded little nowhere town, a gentle young man and a weary young woman sought a place of rest and the sound they heard was that of "No Room."

So tonight, my friends, I say thank you. Thank you for allowing me to experience a night in the heart of family, though my relatives live far away. Thank you for scooting over, patting the seat next to you and offering me a place close by. Thank you for sharing your lives, your laughter, your tears and your joy with me. Thank you for showing me how blessed I am and how generously God lavishes His love on the earth today. Thank you for being tenderhearted, kind, compassionate and faithful to one another. But most of all, tonight I thank you that you are a family that always makes room.

    I love you dearly.

"and she gave birth to her firstborn, a son. She wrapped him in cloths and placed him in a manger, because there was no guest room available for them."
Luke 2: 7

IN PROCESS

For he will be like a refiner's fire or a launderer's soap. He will sit as a refiner and purifier of silver; he will purify the Levites and refine them like gold and silver. Then the LORD will have men who will bring offerings in righteousness, and the offerings of Judah and Jerusalem will be acceptable to the LORD, as in days gone by, as in the former years.
Malachi 3: 2-4

I have been thinking about the Refiner's Fire lately – probably because I feel like I have been in one for some time now.

When I was a little girl, we loved to make homemade ice cream at my granny's house. We did it the hard way, with an old hand cranked ice cream mixer. It seemed like it took forever on those hot summer days. That ice cream just did not want to freeze! I would turn and turn until I thought my arm would surely fall off. "Granny! Granny! How long's this gonna take?" I'd fuss. "I reckon it's gonna take as long as it takes." Would always be her reply.

It was not what I wanted to hear, but it was true. The work just takes however long it takes. You cannot predict when ice cream will freeze in the summer, and unfortunately you cannot predict how long the Refiners fire will have to burn before the work is completed. One thing you can be sure of, however, is that the Refiner never leaves the fire unattended. As children, we knew that if we left the ice cream and ran off to play – it took longer. The work that had been accomplished up to that point then had to be redone.

By the same token, if we run from the flames and reject His purifying process – we just might find ourselves in the same flame at a future date.

God always finishes what He starts.

Did you know that if you do not put your trust in the Refiner and stay committed to the completed work, all the flames will bring about is a brittle hardness? You place something in an oven long enough, it is eventually reduced to ashes, but long before the ash result, there is a hardening process. In both cases, the work is incomplete.

We have seen it time after time. Someone goes through a hard time and a difficult place and instead of being refined, they come away bitter and hard, and do not want to let anyone in. The refining process was not accepted, and therefore the hardness of heart merely increased. Ashes, therefore, mark their path, and most who come in contact with them feel the sting of their dry places.

Oh, dear ones, stay in the process until the work is completed. I know the temperature is rising, and your metal is being tested, but beauty truly is on the way. Do not run. Keep your mind centered on the Refiner instead of the fire. He will keep you in perfect peace – no matter how hot it gets!

And when the work is done...find a nice shade tree and have that bowl of ice cream.

UNRAVELLED

I think I must be tired. I'm not sure.

If I could sit down for a few minutes and actually think, I might be able to figure it out. Lately it seems as if the moment I sit down the phone rings or the doorbell dings. This causes me to entertain the thought that my phone and doorbell are somehow attached to the seat of my comfy chair in the corner. But, it cannot be true, for others sit in that chair and there is no knock at the door for hours on end.

I have noticed that my email message board constantly reminds me that it is time to archive old items... which means there are way too many messages stored in its finite memory. I have decided that my computer and I have the same problem. Too many messages, so little space. My email inbox stays full, and I am quite sure there are many of you sitting out there wondering... (Just like the line from Dances with Wolves)... *Why don't she write?*

I truly do mean to. I have every intention of doing so - soon. I am trusting that all of you who know me have already reached the conclusion that I do love you, and will, therefore, extend me a bit of grace. Those who do not know me... well, I will answer yours first, for I do not expect that same grace extension from you. In time, you may be asked to extend, but for now, just let me say, "The response is in the mail."

Why do I ramble on with such nonsense? Many have asked that question. But what I find is that my mental meanderings are something of an unwinding for me. If you can for one moment picture a huge ball of yarn rolling across a polished floor, leaving its singular threaded trail, you will understand my rambling. It is as if I have wound myself around something important, and must unravel to get at the hidden center.

So what is hidden today that has prompted this trail of twine? Let's see, I must push just a bit to straighten that last bit of unruly thread.

Ah, yes, there it is.

I see it clearly now.

Four little letters: sert; no, ters, wait…estr…

Oh, there it is…

Rest.

I must unravel to rest. I must unwind and rest. I must meander to find my place of rest.

The Father speaks, "*Rest, child.*" The words cause me to breathe deep. "*Rest, child.*" My shoulders relax, my head bent forward, I test the neck muscles with a slow side-to-side stretch.

"*Rest, Child.*"

Head in my hands, my eyes begin to feel their own weight. Like a soft wind blowing through the trees, His voice disturbs me beautifully, "*Rest, child.*"

One more breath; it reaches deep and sends the yarn spinning forward, one single strand meets four letters…

And I rest.

"Come to me. Get away with me and you'll recover your life. I'll show you how to take a real rest. Walk with me and work with me—watch how I do it. Learn the unforced rhythms of grace."
Matthew 11:28 (Message)

WHEN YOU KNOW

Jesus declared, Believe me woman, a time is coming when you will worship the Father neither on this mountain nor in Jerusalem. You Samaritans worship what you do not know; we worship what we do know, for salvation is from the Jews. Yet a time is coming and has now come when the true worshipers will worship the Father in Spirit and truth, for they are the kind of worshipers the Father seeks. God is spirit, and His worshipers must worship in spirit and in truth.

John 4:21-26

Today I am pondering worship.

What actually sent me on this journey was a dream (I know big shock) that brought a quickening revelation to my own heart. For, while I have found my place at His feet for years, I have struggled to explain to people with any type of clarity or accuracy, what worship really means in my life. But the Lord crystallized the heart of a true worshiper for me in one simple yet profound moment.

In this dream I stood on the side of a dusty road that led into Jerusalem. I stood with a crowd of people as they waited on something (or someone). There was a great sense of anticipation and agitated expectancy. They peered down the road, trying to position themselves to see further. Then, from a short distance away I could hear the crowd begin to cheer. It was like the roar of an ocean wave moving in our direction. The words became clearer as they rolled in, "Hosanna!" they cried in their excitement, "Hosanna!"

I realized that (in this dream) I was standing with the crowd as Jesus made His triumphal entry. The shouts continued and rose as the crowd became more jubilant, and many threw their robes and cloaks in the road before Him. Palm branches waved in homage. They shouted in joy, shouted out of emotion, shouted in group camaraderie, shouted as moved by the circumstances, and shouted at His very presence.

Yes, the service was in full motion...

Then I heard her.

I heard something other.

I heard a sound that pierced through the rest. It was verdantly sweet and resonated in a way that made it distinct and precious among the cacophony of increasing noise. It possessed a quality, a tone, a knowing, unlike any of the others. *Though her words were the same, she sang a different song.* It was a singular voice crying out, drenched with tears, and bathed in deep and sorrowful joy.

I watched as this woman threw her ragged cloak at His feet. "Hosanna!" She cried. And her cries rent the atmosphere. "Hosanna!" Her tears wet the earth, each one reverberating beneath my feet, and all I could do was gasp for breath.

And then the dream shifted from the crowd into the very content of her heart. In the depths of the spirit of this woman lay a story, a story of being dragged into the street in her shame and degradation and being forced to stand before the angry, the judging, the religious and pious, who weighed her in the scales and found her wanting. I saw within her heart a story of stones aimed and ready to be released… and then I saw those eyes. Eyes that looked at her with kindness. Eyes that saw ***her;*** not what she had done. I saw within her, all that had touched her ears: the anger, the disgust, the names, the threats, the ridicule, the distaste, the condescension, the insults… all repeating what she already believed about herself. Expecting to feel the first stone strike, she heard instead His voice…*Let the sinless throw the first stone*…and then the sound of stones dropping at the feet of her accusers.

"Woman where are your accusers?" "*Lord, I have none…*" "*Neither do I condemn you…*" and in that moment a Hosanna! was born in the heart of *one who knew*.

And now, I stood beside her understanding why her "Hosanna" was different, why it rang above all of the rest. It came from a heart that had absolutely found its Truth; a heart that resounded with everything she now knew about herself and the Lover of her soul. She did not cry out because everyone else cried out. She did not shout out of emotion or prompted by habit. She did nothing out of the shallows or because it was what she had been taught to do. She cried out from a place of *life-altering personal revelation*. Her worship was a deep honoring and reverencing of His work in her life. Her worship told her story...and His story. She worshiped from a spirit that acknowledged what she knew...He loved her. He covered her. He had become everything to her. She *worshiped Him* completely because she *knew*.

Then I heard a little boy's voice; it rang with the same truth. His heart relived a time of being thrown into the fire by demons, of seizures and fear, then the voice of a man saying, *"I will..."* His truth was a life of possession now given way to a life of freedom. *His hosanna rang true.* He worshiped in spirit and in truth.

What they offered was *Tehillah*- A spontaneous new song. A song that abides in your heart that only you can give words to. It is a song offered straight to God. She Tehillahed God and Tehillah is the praise that God inhabits. It is your heart song. Tehillah is praise offered from your deepest level of recognized truth, and in that place, God takes up residence.

Only when our worship becomes deeply honest can we enter into the "spirit and truth" that God desires. When we can begin to sing a spontaneous song from a place inside of us *that knows*- that really knows, then, and only then, do we shift from being a house that has a lot of good singers and talented musicians, and even anointed gifts, to a house that He inhabits. Because if the praise that He inhabits is Tehillah praise (the praise that enthrones Him is our personal, spontaneous, spirit birthed song), then when we get to that place of honesty within ourselves, that pristine acknowledgment of God from our depths, He inhabits. And in that, we become like the woman on the side of the road, whose sound was different from all of the rest.

Oh guys, do you understand that when spirit marries truth, the offspring is a new song, the child is Tehillah worship. Can I tell you something else? You can have great passion and no truth. You can sing louder, run faster, jump higher, shout most radically, run the aisles and never get honest.

Passion does not equal true worship.

You see, Jesus told the woman at the well that a day was coming when it did not matter where you worshiped, but then the intimation of the next sentence often gets brushed past. He said, "You Samaritans worship what you do not know... we **worship what we know**... for Salvation is from the Jews." In other words, the day is coming when you too will enter into a place of worshiping because *you know* the truth, and when that happens, it is not going to matter where you are. When you worship because you really *know*... you now enter into the land of spirit and truth. We are not talking about praise here. We are talking about the sound of a testimony. The sound of awakening on levels we've never touched or heard before... the singing of the soul.

Friends, praise can issue from a feeling, an emotion, a delight, a stirring, an experience, but worship must flow from truth.

What I want to propose to you and offer up for your consideration is that the missing element of our worship in this day is truth. It is the element that takes us from being a good church to a kingdom mover. It is the element that changes everything.

Across the land there are churches built upon and steeped in worship arts. Dynamic sounds issue from the houses; singers unparalleled in gifts, musicians unequaled. The call has gone out and dancers have struck their rhythm. Praise pounds through the atmosphere, and could we be a listener above the earth on a Sunday morning, we would hear a chorus, a symphony of exaltation lifting from this blue orb.

Still, while we have pushed and pressed our way into the *sound* of heaven, there is a note missing, a tone we long for that would cause all to ring and resound. It is that tone, that ring, that melody, which will shift us from one level of offering to the next. I believe that sound is Truth. Honest worship.

For so many years we have danced upon the "in spirit" part of this instruction. We, as good Evangelicals, know how to move in the spirit... or at least we think we do. Nobody gets *into the spirit* like a charismatic (in our opinion - oops! sarcasm). Ah, yes, we know about the spirit. We can get into the spirit - the spirit of the experience, the spirit of joy, the spirit of anticipation, the spirit of expectation. We can work up a great spiritual praise experience. But in order for it to pass the point of praise and enter into clearly delineated worship, deep and profound truth must be added to the equation. And truth requires some transparency we prefer to dance ourselves out of.

You see, while your praise may speak to your level of involvement and passion, your worship speaks to the level of true revelation in your life. It speaks to what *you know* about Him. Your worship tells your story. It is your testimony fleshed out…for better or for worse. You can praise Him. You can sing. You can dance. You can shout. You can enjoy. You can be saved. You can be a good Christian. You can be a Pastor, teacher, missionary, praise leader, and effective witness. You can be many good things without deep revelation, but you will never be a true worshiper until you can worship Him in Spirit *and Truth.*

Everything about someone entering into true worship testifies. Their worship acknowledges, it awakens, it pierces, it penetrates. *True worship is resonant and resident.* True worship has a story. True worship has a dance. True worship has a scent, a tone, a fragrance… a voice unlike any other. Worship is birthed in your life when your God becomes very real to you, when you finally get the hugeness of what He has done in and for you, and begin to understand how undeserving you are of that goodness. Only revelation can birth that in your life. And when you know…I mean really know…Your soul sings.

A DIFFERENT INTERCESSION

In 1990 I encountered something truly life altering. I was in a church in Oak Ridge, Tennessee, playing piano for an altar service when I heard the most devastatingly painful and intimate sound. I heard a moan that made the hair stand up on the back of my neck and tears immediately come to my eyes. My breath caught in my throat, and my hands literally froze on the piano keys, as a beautiful young woman to my right buckled over in anguish and groan after groan began to rack her frail body, issuing forth from the very depths of her being.

I had never heard anything like it.

I tried to breathe, but the groaning of the

woman was shaking my spirit in a way I couldn't understand. I could not catch my breath, but instead gulped in air like a woman drowning. Tears coursed down my cheeks as I watched her, people gathered around her, but it was as if they could not touch her... not for fear, but out of reverence for a profoundly sacred moment.

She was in the grip of God. An intercession of soul was taking place, and we were stunned by the depth and breadth of what was taking place in the spirit realm right in front of our eyes.

"God", I asked, "what is happening?" I asked because it was an automatic response, though my spirit had already bore witness to the truth of what was taking place. Still, He spoke to my heart in confirmation, "*She is in deep intercession. My Spirit intercedes with groans and utterance. She does not know how to pray through the devastated places.*"

The Holy Spirit was making intercession for a heart that could not find the words to voice its pain. She was broken, and only God could give utterance to her pain. The intercession of groaning was planted in my spirit in that moment.

Nineteen years later, I still shake on the inside when I think about that moment.

I would later find out that the beautiful young mother had lost her husband that week. Still, raw with loss, she stood in the altar with all of her pain, and all of devastation, not knowing how to release it to God. So, God did what God does, He searched her heart and the Holy Spirit made intercession in a way she could not understand.

I was changed in that moment, for I knew God had allowed me to witness the use of a tool I had not known existed before then. I had heard all of the teaching and even knew the scriptures, but my working knowledge of the scripture at that point had stopped with the praying in tongues portion. But you see, God knew that a day would come in my life when I would come before Him with great need and no words to utter... so He prepared me in advance, showing me that when I needed Him desperately, He would move through me and release my cries through groanings.

Now, this place of groaning has become a place of breakthrough for me. You may never need it, but I definitely have. When I feel a pulling in the spirit and the heaviness of intercession begins to draw me, I inevitably find myself in this place. It is a hard but good place. It is a place of deep spiritual communion, and I also believe it is a place of spiritual birthing. And for me, these groanings have been clarion cries ushering in many deep transitional seasons.

I do not know how God will use this weapon in your life, or even if He will. You may never choose to pick it up and use it. But I can tell you beyond a shadow of a doubt that it has been the intercession of groaning that has changed everything about how I pray. If I am frustrated, instead of getting up and walking out of my prayer time, I am able to press deeper. If I am hurt or wounded and words are not sufficient, I find release in this kind of pouring out.

Scripture tells us that there were times when the prophets would call for the wailing women to make the difference in the situation. I believe it is such a time. I believe there is much wordless intercession to be made…and He is looking for those who are willing to use this tool of groaning. Even if you never use it… at least you now know that it exists.

If you want to research it, please read Romans 8. If you want to allow God to show you firsthand, there is only one way...

Can I get an *Ahhhhhhhh Jesus!*

Meanwhile, the moment we get tired in the waiting, God's Spirit is right alongside helping us along. If we don't know how or what to pray, it doesn't matter. He does our praying in and for us, making prayer out of our wordless sighs, our aching groans.
Romans 8:26 (Message)

THE BIGGEST CHANGE OF ALL

Can I talk to you about the most extreme change God has brought in my life? There are so many, but it really isn't hard to choose. And though I know most would automatically say their biggest change or transformation was in their salvation, I cannot really say that. I know this may sound strange, but you see, I am a preacher's kid and I gave my heart to Jesus so early in life that I didn't *feel* a huge yoke fall away. I had no time to actually be terribly bad before I asked Him to be my Savior. Do you see what I am saying? I mean, yes, spiritual transformation took place, but in this flesh, I experienced little change.

Still, I could offer you many other wonderful changes; the change from fearing God's wrath to experiencing His goodness (huge); from feeling like a failure to believing I could do anything God asked me to do (phenomenal); or delivering me from years of bulimia (life-changing); or setting me free from wrong mindsets because of abuse I experienced as a child (can I get a witness?). There have been so many wonderful changes in my life because of God. I could truly never name them all. But I have to say the most stunningly miraculous thing He has done in this life is teach me a new way to love. He has literally enlarged my capacity to really love. Not Him. I have always loved Him like crazy. But He changed me most when He opened my heart to *love His people.*

Now, I know that may sound strange to you, and in all honesty, it seemed strange to me at the time. I had been serving God for 35 years, teaching, leading ministries, working in high-level positions- all *for God*, and out of my love *for God*. So when He began to deal with this part of my life, I was shocked. I thought this was one area that was actually in good shape. I did not know that I needed to be transformed in my love walk, because I was always doing stuff for *His people*, always busy, always pouring, and always surrounded by the work of the ministry. But through a series of events and personal revelations, the Lord began to show me that if I were to truly be about His business, I would have to be about His people.

My first clue that something was off center was when I went to a training seminar with one of my friends and co-leaders. We sat down in the back and began to listen to the teacher. It was great, right up until the time he said…"Now, let's break into groups of three or four and have some discussion time…Oh, and do not stay with the people you came with." I thought I was going to be sick. It was a revelation. I could easily stand in front of a thousand people and talk about Jesus and not bat an eyelash. But the one on one, face to face, made me break out in hives.

Then a little while later, the Lord began to point some small things out to me, like how I would leave skid marks getting out the side door after I would speak at an event. Or how I would leave people asking, "Where'd she go?" And after particularly bombarded times or a conference with long prayer lines, I would retreat for days. I thought I was tired, but I was actually just in hiding.

It's funny now, because if you had asked me, I would have told you I was very sociable, very approachable, very available, very caring... but what I was, was afraid. I wanted to offer God to everyone, but none of myself, because in truth, if I offered me and they did not like me, I was way too insecure to deal with the rejection. So, I delivered God's message, but fell short of offering God's heart.

Then one day at a conference in Missouri, standing in front of thousands, the Lord did something. As I watched the women sing and worship, and cry and sway, God opened my eyes. In the briefest of moments and the most profound of glimpses, He opened a window for me in the spirit and allowed me the tiniest foray into His love for the people who stood in that room. The most brief fragrance of God-love and it completely took my breath away and absolutely buckled my knees. I felt like I had been hit with a sledgehammer.

I had never experienced anything like it.

The best way I could describe it would be to

take that first night in the hospital, when you held your baby for the very first time in the quiet and stillness of the room… when you looked at their face and were absolutely overwhelmed with the awe, the responsibility, the intense and possessive love that only the one who carried and delivered can feel… that amazing and scary love… and now multiply it until the breath leaves your body.

That is God love. I cried the ugly cry until I could not cry anymore. My eyes were swollen, my head hurt, and people were walking several paces ahead of me pretending not to hear my wailing, but none of it mattered, because God had given me revelation. Painful, repentance inducing revelation, and I felt as if I would never see the world in the same way. And I can honestly tell you I never have.

That glimpse of God's love shook everything I thought I knew about myself. That glimpse lifted years of Christian veneer off of my life. All of the religiosity fell off. All of the lingo I had learned, all of the methods and patterns and habits just came unglued in that moment.

And I cried. I just thought I had cried before,

but God changed me that night. He got into rooms in my heart that I did not even know existed and cleaned house. It was just the most painfully glorious thing I have ever experienced with Him. He emptied me, and then He did the most marvelous thing, like a breath sweeping the room, He filled me with a new capacity for God-love. He so messed me up.

I am different. My life is different. It is crazy different. I walk through much of it feeling like a fingernail torn into the quick, but it is such a good pain, because I have finally found His heart – *and it is you.*

My friends, if you are looking for Him, if you are searching for the heart of God, look beside you. Go horizontal.

I think one of the most profound things the Father shared with me about this was a simple illustration. I have three children, Aaron (25), Matthew (22), and Kayti (15). They are my heart. Aaron and Matthew have my wild hair and warped sense of humor. Kayti has a wicked awesome wit, my teenage form and my expressive eyebrows. When they enter a room, my breath catches. I would without hesitation die for any one of them. They are mine. They are me.

Now...you may think you love me, and even tell me you love me, but if you see Aaron, Matt, or Kayti on the side of the road and you know them to be my children, and do not stop to help them, your actions expose your heart. If you can pass them by, I no longer believe you when you say you love me. Because if you love me – really love me – you know how I feel about them – and will love them.

It is so simple it is hard.

We know that we have passed from death to life, because we love our brothers. Anyone who does not love remains in death. Anyone who hates his brother is a murderer, and you know that no murderer has eternal life in him. This is how we know what love is: Jesus Christ laid down his life for us. And we ought to lay down our lives for our brothers. If anyone has material possessions and sees his brother in need but has no pity on him, how can the love of God be in him? Dear children, let us not love with words or tongue but with actions and in truth. This then is how we know that we belong to the truth, and how we set our hearts at rest in his presence.
I John 3:14-19

I can honestly tell you that the most extreme

makeover I have been through in my life is that His people now break my heart for a completely different reason. I no longer sneak out the side door and I no longer hide in the back. God has opened my arms, and opened my heart. It is the most amazing thing imaginable to me that God can give you a love for people that you never knew existed, and in that... I truly know I have passed from death to life.

And oh what a life it is.

IN THIS SEASON

I have been doing some thinking this week. I know, it's enough to make your head hurt, but I just could not help myself. I was reading a small, insignificant little book and one of the lines in the book planted a hook deep within my spirit. It simply said, *"For most of human history life was measured and lived by season, not time."* When I read it I had a flash of one of my husband's westerns - one Indian explaining to the other *"My son has seen 12 summers..."* - a life being recorded by season. It seems a little strange given our obsession with seconds, minutes, hours, days, weeks, months, timeframes and deadlines, but it was a very accurate measure of one's life. I cannot explain it, but something inside of me quickened when I thought about this concept, for something deep within all of us battles the swift passage of time. We race against it, try to find ways to turn it back, and continually complain that we do not know where it all went. Ah, but if life is measured in seasons, not in seconds, now that is a different story. Seasons give you a much broader picture.

I have decided that when I look in the mirror, I will see the beautiful passing of seasons etched upon my face. I will not abhor time and its ravages, but will embrace the transformation and progression of my seasons. While I may look back and see *time* that has been wasted, lamenting its loss, I will not scorn my seasons, for my seasons have been immersed in tranquil waters and blazing fires. My seasons have surrounded me, carrying me into laughter, tears, empathy, excruciating clarity and simple faith. Time has not marked my course, but my seasons have. There are childish seasons, coming of age seasons, pain-filled seasons, and seasons of joy, seasons of serenity, seasons of turmoil, seasons of alone*ness*, seasons of hospitality, seasons of stagnation and seasons of abounding growth.

So many seasons, so little time.

Today, I am going to focus on my season. I want to really be aware of where I am and what God is doing. I have determined that I will not mourn for seasons past, but will fully live in the season God has moved me into. I will not cling to the ideas, positions, tasks, articles, possessions, and even ministries of seasons gone by, but will open my hands and release them as God says move forward. (Somehow that is much easier to do when you no longer enjoy the season you are in, the problem comes when God says you are entering a new season and you were very comfortable in your old one.)

So, what do you do when it hurts to leave your season? You do it anyway. Heart bleeding, tears falling, you bruise your knees one more time and press your face into His chest as you give Him your yes. Another season etches its way upon your countenance, and your fingers relax their grip on the past as your feet find His rhythm. Green grass gives way to crunchy, colorful leaves, and the warm summer breeze takes on autumn's crisp fragrance.

Morning Mist

The colors become more vibrant, there is an extravagant appreciation for what was always there, but somehow escaped your notice, and you walk face-first into your most beautiful season... Until the next one comes along.

*To everything there is a season,
and a time to every purpose under the heaven.
Ecclesiastes 3:1 (KJV)*

STILL ANSWERING

What do you do when you simply cannot find the words to tell Him how much you love Him? How do you sing a song to Him that only your heart knows? How do you lay out before Him, your soul open and longing for His touch, waiting for what you cannot even name? That's where I am today. I find myself so completely and beautifully broken before this God that I love. I am at once ready to cry and moved to laughter.

Overwhelmed.

Yes, that is it. I am overwhelmed. His goodness has gripped me, His heartbeat resounds in my ears, and I feel His breath winding through my spirit.

Oh, I love how He messes me up. Mascara streaks my face as Kleenex form tiny Ebenezer's all around this well-worn carpet. Just when I think I am fully unraveled and ready to sit upright, I feel that tight grabbing in the pit of my stomach and I buckle once again as His presence rocks my world. How foolish to think He was done with this work.

Face down I teeter between heaven and cool linoleum.

One prayer. One small sentence. I should have known He was listening. This ongoing revelation of lesser gods, and small pursuits; the painful disintegration of what I thought I knew. It brings me to but one conclusion: God is answering my unconscious prayer; "Father, let there be less of me and more of You."

It sounded great at the time, somewhat holy in fact, for the emphasis in my mind was upon the *more of you* part. Foolishly we think that more of Him is easily placed on top of what already exists within us. However, somewhere between the carpet fibers and eternity, the emphasis flew onto the wrong words, and wound up on the *less of me* part.

And He just keeps answering.

As I move through prayer into the Holy Places of His Presence, I am painfully aware that there is so much still to surrender. My hands clutch in a useless attempt to hide this heart and all of its shallowness.

In His faithfulness, He allows me brief glimpses of my various vanities before He steps in and covers me, reminding me that He is enough…and less is inevitably coming.

How could I ask for more?

To everything there is a season,
and a time to every purpose under the heaven.
Ecclesiastes 3:1 (KJV)

TRUST ME

It is a funny thing, this need to hide ourselves from others. I sat this morning pondering an email I had gotten from a close friend. You know the kind of friend that speaks honestly and you have to receive it because you know it is done in love. In the email I had been admonished to expand my borders... come out of my comfort zone. My initial response was not pretty. It is amazing how quickly you can send a letter across wires and airspace. Unfortunately, that same technology prohibits the withdrawal of said letter once you have come to your senses.

Anyway, I digress...I sent off the letter pointing out all of the ways I have expanded my borders and stepped out of my comfort zone. I will give you a brief glimpse into the letter:

"I have broadened my comfort zone about all I can handle this year. I have actually been nice to people I do not know, and opened my home to those who openly dislike me. I have prayed for those who curse me (as they curse me...), sat patiently (without interrupting) through dissertations on all of my faults – as viewed by whomever was speaking at the time (waiting until I was alone with my Father before exposing the gaping wounds). I have scrubbed toilets in Missions, cleaned the hair of strangers out of bathtubs I would never bathe in, painted nurseries, rocked babies, been spit up on, provided taxi service to those who needed a ride to church, and even spent time under the pews seeking God for His heart concerning this body you seem to think I hide from...

I have cried with the mourners, rejoiced with the giddy ... I have run screaming from my comfort zone this year, feet set on fire- just because He called me out of it. My pegs have been lengthened, my chords strengthened.

If you have seen me in my comfort zone of

late, it is a most rare glimpse you have caught – kind of like a sighting of Bigfoot or the Loch Ness Monster. People say these things exist, but I am not so sure..."

As you can see, I was not having one of my better moments. As I recited my perceived accomplishments, typing faster than my sane fingers normally move, smoke lifting from the keyboard as I put on paper what I would not have voiced aloud, I paid no attention to the still small voice that whispered through my spirit. The Spirit's words moved though me like a wind that twists through the trees…soft, gentle, but somehow beautifully disruptive. Typing faster and louder to drown out the Spirit wind, I stopped only when the send button clicked off in my ears, a resounding Uh-Oh echoing in the pit of my stomach. I knew that somewhere in cyberspace a mouthy redhead had gone over the edge, and soon a friend would be forced (by her words) to tread that edge with her.

Fools care nothing for thoughtful discourse; all they do is run off at the mouth.
Proverbs 18:2 (Message)

My office silent, I stared at the screen before me. The Wind-Word flowed through me again. Rustling my branches...*A small risk...You know I want more*...AAAAHHH! Stop it! Whistle, sing, clog, just don't listen to the wind. (Fingers in the ears do nothing to stop the inner voice) La la la la – la la la la (most effective when done to the tune of the Twilight Zone). Shuffle the paper on the desk; make as much noise as possible. *You know I want more*...I distinctly hear Charlie Brown's yell as Lucy pulls the football away and sends him flying. I picture myself laying on my back in the grass, staring at the sky; my posterior bruised, my ego tattered, contemplating the same questions he must have posed, *Am I really here again*?

I am not an unfriendly sort; I am more the "I like my space" sort. I can stand in front of a thousand people and talk about Jesus and never give it a second thought. But put me in a room with three people and ask me to sit down and talk, my mouth goes dry, my stomach knots, and the spirit of Lance Armstrong overtakes me and I start looking for a bicycle.

I remember one particular instance where my

friend Mary and I were asked to attend a class in Nashville one evening. I was fine with it until we walked into this room full of nice people who actually wanted to speak to me. I practically sat in Mary's lap trying to find my comfort zone. I had almost started to breathe normally when the leader said, *"Let's break up into groups of four... do not stay with the people you came with."*

The room spun.

I am quite certain the fingernail scars on Mary's arm will one day heal, but let's just say I went reluctantly. My group of four was about halfway up toward the front of the room, and Mary's was in the back.

While I did my best to participate in the group, I found that my one syllable monotone answers did not contribute much to the discussion format. I also found out that nervously rocking your foot back and forth with great fury can actually move your chair across the floor to the back of the room without ever having to stand, and can eventually put you smack dab in the middle of the group you wanted to be with in the first place.

Anyway… let's just say this mountain has been one I have hidden behind before.

Please do not misunderstand me. I truly do love people. I try not to sit in judgment, or walk in criticism of others. I know how weak I am, and I recognize my own frailties to the point that I would never want to walk mercilessly through life. It is probably that very recognition of self that makes me want to run from intimate encounters.

What some may perceive to be arrogance is, nine times out of ten, insecurity. We are so afraid of letting someone get to know us. We reject others before they get a chance to reject us. We have this tape that runs though our minds telling us, don't open up… you will get hurt… you will be judged. Unfortunately, many times that is true. You do get hurt. But loving well is worth the risk.

What if Jesus had withheld His heart, but gone to the cross out of duty? What if He had done what He had to do, but never touched the lives of the people? What if He had sat down during His forty day fast that preceded His ministry, and said *Okay, Father, I will do what you've asked me to do. I will fully PERFORM my duties, but I will not love them because You and I both know they are going to break my heart.*

Can you imagine the absurdity of a life spent in duty and service without love? Can you imagine Jesus lifting Mary Magdalene from the dirt and briskly saying, "You're forgiven. Don't do it anymore," and turning His back on her hearts greatest need, love manifested? It's called performance without love, duty without passion. We do it every day.

So, how do we make the decision to live in this land called Vulnerable? The answer may sound way too simple, but when I pray about this very issue in my own life I hear Him say, "Trust Me." (…And Lucy places the football on the ground, holding it with one finger…the challenge clear in her laughing eyes…) Unfortunately, my response to the Father is usually the same. Trust You? Lord, You know I trust You. It's everyone else I have a problem with. His gentle rebuke is the same…Trust Me.

I may not be the smartest of women, but I know full well what He is saying with those two words. "Trust Me" in God-speak, is followed by the unmistakable words *even when it hurts.* I originally thought the phrase was *if* it hurts, but I am quite positive the word is when. It is inevitable. Hearts without walls are subject to the occasional arrow.

I have come to one wall-shattering conclusion. My issues with people have everything to do with my trust in Him. (Can you say Ouch! Hallelujah?) If I trust Him and His plan for my life, I can love you in spite of the risk to myself. Self...oh, here we go...

Though He slay me, yet, will I trust in Him,
Job 13:15 (KJV)

Back to self...

And he said, I heard thy voice in the garden, and I was afraid, because I was naked; and I hid myself.
Genesis 3:10 (KJV)

We have had the same problem for thousands of years. We see our own nakedness and we hide. We see our own vulnerabilities and we jump behind the nearest fig tree. The only problem is that we now do it because of man instead of God. If I let you see my scars, will they be all you see? If the pedestal wobbles, and we topple to the ground, will there be hands that extend to help us up, or laughter that judges?

We all walk these roads. We all ponder these things in our hearts. We fight the urge to open up and draw close to another human being, by denying our need to do so. We do exactly what I did when I heard the Wind-Word shifting and turning in my own spirit… we put our hands over our hearts and begin to dance a dance borne of duty instead of joy. We dance and perform with tears streaming down our spirits. We sing a silent song of desperation as our hearts pound within us. We deny our need for contact by performing to the point of exhaustion. We numb ourselves by doing the right thing for all the wrong reasons. We have become much like Pinocchio, our arms attached to strings of fear; we dance about, silly smiles painted on our faces, when the cry of our heart is… *I want to be real*…I want to be real. But what does that mean?

The best definition I came up with was "Not

fake…without the commitment of fraud." Can we go there? Can we be who we are without fear? My answer is (sorry) probably not. I know the Scriptures say that perfect love casts out fear, but I am not there yet. I am not so sure I will ever get there on this planet. It is going to take a lot of "perfected love" for me to live without fear of letting down my walls. However, that does not mean I will not let them down. I will just have to do it afraid.

I can choose to put myself on that limb if I know the limb is where He wants me to be.

Take the thousand and give it to the one who risked the most. And get rid of this "play-it-safe" who won't go out on a limb.
Matthew 25:28 (Message)

So, here I am once again, lying in the grass, the football nowhere to be seen. I can lay here for a while and contemplate, but I do not like ants and various critters taking liberties with my being. Nor do I like the feeling of my skin being parched by the sun. If I stay here much longer I will be red faced and thoroughly chewed up

(*Selah*).

Yes, I have a choice to make. The question streaks across the sky like a Lobster Shack advertisement at the beach...*DO I RISK IT? DO I RISK IT?*

Do I run at this relationship thing full force and take the risk of never even making a connection? Do I move to the land of Vulnerable and pitch my tent on the banks of the River Available? I mean, this letting-people-into-our-lives business can be extremely scary. It means making phone calls I do not want to make, babysitting when I would rather not, listening when I would rather talk, and being teachable when I think I know it all. It means forgiving when I want to hide and lick my wounds. Do I really want to live there again?

I ponder a moment longer, searching the clouds above. In my mind's eye I see friends sitting at my table laughing with me. I see Christine standing by my bedside holding Kayti in her arms for the first time, bringing me chocolate... just because; I see Dawn standing by the piano, smiling at me, tears in her eyes, as she patiently listens to another one of my trial tunes… just because; I see Anna literally taking the shirt off her back (she had two on at the time) and loaning it to my nine year old daughter so she can wear it to school the next day, …just because.

Then it hits me, all of these just becauses, all of these blessings in my life, they came at a cost, and the cost was being willing to take the risk. These beautiful friends put themselves out there and took the risk of sharing their lives with me. I am blessed because of it. They made the decision that the reward outweighed the fear and that God-relationships were worth it. They trusted Him and let me in.

I know the answer now.

The Wind Word has completed His beautiful disruption, leaving me with the assurance that the risk is His, and love is always worth it.

I hear the faint cry of the commander of an ant army, *"Over here!"* Followed by the sound of ant feet running through the grass. I have to get up. I rub my eyes and glance one last time into the sky above me. There, upon the cool blue canvas, billowy white clouds shift and roll with the wind. I watch as they take on the fluffy but distinct form of (yes, you guessed it) a football.

Somewhere in the deep laughing part of my spirit, I hear His voice laced with humor say…*Trust me?*

Then he reassured her: "Courage, daughter. You took a risk of faith, and now you're well."
Matthew 9:21 (Message)

GREAT THINGS

I spoke with a friend this evening who was quite frustrated. She had various things going on in her life and I sat down to talk and pray with her, praying for peace and comfort, and that God would continue to use her in great ways in the Kingdom. After I prayed for her, she brought my attention back to the words of my prayer. She said, "You know, so many people have spoken that over me. They have said I would do great things with my life; things that I cannot even see." She shook her head as if to say, well, it hasn't happened yet. She looked at me and said, "I don't know what He's waiting for. I mean, I am ready! When am I going to start to do these great things?"

I looked at this sweet, sweet, woman and thought to myself, she doesn't see that she is already walking in the great. You see, asleep on the seat next to her was a baby – not her own – that she has taken to heart and loves like it is her own. As she talked with me about those future "great things" her hand unconsciously went to the tiny arm of the baby and patted. As she vocalized her concerns, her hand adjusted the little covers on the child… a child whose mother was not around. The baby's soft curls strayed toward her little lips and the woman gently brushed the curls back. "When will God use me to do great things?"

My heart melted.

Oh, my precious friends, can't you see that the great is in the small. Great is found in selfless acts that are automatic and unplanned. Great is found in this very moment and lasts for eternity. Great is picking up tiny socks and putting them on tiny flat feet. Great is kissing a cheek that has tootsie roll on it and not making a face or running your hand across your mouth. Great is in touching the hand of a friend who just needs to know you are there. Great is found in compassionate tears and empathetic groanings. Great is found in the places we never think to look; here and now... in the small, silent, unremarkable moments that silently and profoundly change the lives of the unsuspecting.

My friend is a woman of greatness. She is selfless and generous of spirit. She is kind and gentle in nature and everything she does is done for others. Her life is spent in the great... only she does not see it. Perhaps that is best, for when we begin to see our works as great, they quickly become quite small in the eyes of the One who truly matters. Beloved, live a life of greatness... today... now!

Also a dispute arose among them as to which of them was considered to be greatest. Jesus said to them, "The kings of the Gentiles lord it over them; and those who exercise authority over them call themselves Benefactors. But you are not to be like that. Instead, the greatest among you should be like the youngest, and the one who rules like the one who serves. For who is greater, the one who is at the table or the one who serves? Is it not the one who is at the table? But I am among you as one who serves.

Luke 22:24-27

Remember: start small.

A GOOD PAIR OF SNEAKERS

Sometimes it's so hard to do what you know you should do – especially when it comes to your flesh. You might walk past a bakery, and suddenly all of your good intentions for that healthy new lifestyle are defeated by the aroma of butter cream frosting.

I am quite sure I have startled a few bakers with my sudden and desperate entrance into their domain. My fingerprints (and a few drool spots) can be found on glass display counters across the Southeast.

Fortunately, you can also find skid marks outside a few of those same establishments, as I made my hasty exit. You see I knew if I allowed myself to linger in the presence of temptation I would soon have powdered sugar on my lips, a dreamy look in my eyes, and a popped button or two.

Temptation will always come at us, but God has given us the marvelous ability to walk away from it. All we have to do is learn to actually tell ourselves no.

Crazy, huh?

Believe it or not, it can be just that easy. We really don't need all of the things we think we need. If children are given whatever they want, whenever they want it they become spoiled and demanding. The same is true of us. If we expect our every desire to be met, if we allow ourselves to think that we must have whatever we want – that we somehow deserve it – it shows up in our attitudes and sometimes our waistlines.

We are very spoiled.

Not good.

Ah, but what a very good God we have. Listen to what He tells us:

The only temptation that has come to you is that which

everyone has. But you can trust God, who will not permit you to be tempted more than you can stand. But when you are tempted, he will also give you a way to escape so that you will be able to stand it.
1 Corinthians 10:13 (NCV)

He is the One Who makes it possible for me to leave those tennis shoe tracks outside the walls of my greatest temptations. God always gives us a way out.

Whatever your temptation; food, drugs, alcohol, pornography, laziness, lying, apathy, or plain old bad attitude…God leaves an open door for you to come out.

My advice?

Keep a good pair of sneakers on hand!

THE COAT

A couple of years ago I had a great coat. Long, black leather, all the way to my ankles. I loved that coat. I thought I looked good in that coat. You could wear that coat over your pajamas and drive your kids to school and no one would know it. It really didn't matter what you wore – as long as you had THE COAT.

You could not wear that coat without strutting just a little bit, without tossing your hair and catching a glimpse of yourself as you happened by mirrors, glass doors, pieces of aluminum foil… I wore the coat proudly – and often. I wore it to the mall, wore it to dinners and parties. Why, I even wore it to church.

That is where it happened.

If I had just not been quite so eager to look cool at church, things might not have turned out like this. I should have worn the plaid cardigan, or the nice warm fleece that Wednesday night – but no...No, that just wasn't cool enough.

I walked up the aisle feeling cool. As I sat with my husband I still felt cool. As the missionary got up to speak, I sat back against my leather coat and thought – *this is cool.* Everything was ultra cool, right up until the time I heard the Holy Spirit say to my heart, "I want you to give your coat to the missionary's wife." I shook my head to clear the obviously insane ramblings. Give away my coat?

HA! Boy, that devil sure is getting good at disguising his voice."

"Give the coat to the missionary's wife."

But God, I began. My voice trembling...*This coat makes me cool. I am pretty sure people look at me and think,* "Wow, look at her, she is so cool!" *This coat makes me feel good, God. This coat is ME...*I argued – still He prompted. This went on throughout the service. I would love to say that at the end of the service I rushed to where the woman stood, but I think we both know better.

My boots peeled rubber on the foyer carpet as I hit warp speed and found myself sitting in the front seat of the car. *Where is my family,* I thought? *No time for fellowship tonight! Why... just look at the time! We have to get home! This is a school night, ya know! I mean, the inconsideration!*

"Take the coat to the missionary's wife," came the spirit-nudge.

Where are those kids? Those kids know they are supposed to come straight to the car.

Hal somehow appeared in the driver's seat, the kids piling in behind. As he started the car and we began to leave the parking lot (almost safe now), I ever so casually mentioned... "You know, (laugh, laugh) I kind of felt, for just a moment, mind you, that just maybe there was the possibility that I was supposed to give my coat to the missionary's wife (more nervous laughter)."

I expected (hoped) that Hal would turn to me and say, "That is an expensive coat! You can't give that coat away."

I should have known better.

The tires squealed as he practically stood the car on its side hanging that U-turn in the parking lot. The car came to a screeching halt right outside the foyer doors…"Well?" He said, looking pointedly at my cool coat.

Fine! I thought. *Just great! Better be careful what you pray for! "I want a husband who is sold out to you, God" I mimicked in my most sarcastic mental voice, as I reached for the door handle.*

I accepted my fate. As I stepped out of the door I am pretty sure I heard a Mozart funeral dirge begin to play in the background. I could have sworn I heard taps coming from the front of the sanctuary as I carried the coat toward the little lady standing by the table in the foyer. I walked forward, the coat held before me as if I were offering gold, frankincense and Myrrh. In my minds eye I saw myself kneeling, head bowed as I as I offered the precious garment.

In actuality, I am pretty sure I shouted something like…"Here! God said I had to give this to you!" as I threw the coat at the woman's head.

I expected the flower petals to begin falling softly around me and choirs of angelic children to begin singing *Hallelujah… Hallelujah.*

What I got instead was a very puzzled look from a little missionary lady, who appeared to be thinking, what in the world do I want with a heavy leather coat in the middle of a tropical climate?

I turned, slinking slowly away, looking decidedly very un-cool. No more pajamas to school. No more cool visions in the aluminum foil around my children's sandwiches.

As I sulked back into the car, family waiting patiently for me to set the example and obey God (I was not a very good one that night), I just could not get the tears out of my eyes or the coat off of my mind. I had to bring it up one more time with my Father, Whom I was not too happy with at the time.

"Fine, God. You wanted her to have the coat; she's got the coat. I hate to tell you this, but I don't think she wanted it."

"Child," He spoke very patiently, with a tinge of laughter in His voice, "that is not the point. *I* wanted the coat."

"Why, God? Why did you want my favorite coat?"

"Because, child," He spoke softly, for my ears alone, "it is time for a new one." And in that moment God began to breathe through my heart as He moved in to begin re-mantling the calling on my life. The coat had merely been a symbol of something (pride, arrogance, insecurity perhaps?) I needed to lay down in order to move forward in Him. He had something else with which to cover me.

Tears slid down my cheeks, as the impact of this mirror-moment hit me. I wept over this stubborn heart of mine, and repented of a nature I hadn't known could be so selfish. As my hard heart broke, I began to pour out its contents before Him. "Oh, Father, forgive me…change me…create in me a pure heart…" As the tears began to slow and my heart began to cleanse, I turned my eyes once again to my

Father.

"I really am sorry, Father."

"I know, Daughter."

And the coat of a child became the mantle of a Daughter, and it slid firmly onto repentant shoulders.

And this is love: that we walk in obedience to his commands. As you have heard from the beginning, his command is that you walk in love.
2 John 1:6

A BEAUTIFUL FALLING

I do not even know where to begin. To say that this has overtaken me would be a grave understatement. For, I cannot begin to fathom and fully plumb the depths of what God has been doing in this battered heart of mine. I am humbled and exhilarated, weepy and caught up in hilarity; I shake my head at what I cannot put my finger on but know full well is there. I suppose, most plainly put, I have fallen in love with Him.

I know, already there are those taking issue with the words *fallen in love,* for that implies an eventual rising out of love. Ah, but this falling has taken some forty-one years, and I do not feel the rising as of yet. Quite to the contrary, I feel the wind on my face as I fall faster and deeper. The world spins by me as my gaze locks with His and I no longer fight this pull toward My Beloved. I have never wanted anything like I want Him, never longed for anything like I long for His Presence. I did not mean to. I did not set out to lose myself. I merely thought to like Him enough to make Him like me. Too late I learned it does not work that way. A gentle wooing, birthed of profound love has set a fire within these bones, and I would have been consumed had I not finally found my face to His chest, my ear to His heartbeat, my breath mingled with His.

Though I do not wish to frighten you with words that evoke such intimate images, I must tell you what I have found in His Presence… this purest of intimacy. His is the take-your-breath-away kind of touch. His is the voice that speaks and drenches your soul with Myrrh, leaving you quite undone. His beauty, fierce and humbling, is that of which dreams could never be made, for He is beyond human dream and thought. He is piercing in intensity, yet completely consuming in His loveliness.

Oh, my friend, I do not know how to write about tears that fall because of unseen beauty, or breath that catches at fragrances no one else can smell. My personal command of the English language is sorely inadequate when attempting to paint the eternal; still I have no recourse but to try. I have no choice, for love compels me to make you painfully, startlingly aware of this life-altering plunge into intimacy with Christ. Beyond the precipice of pews and platforms, hymns, choir lofts and vestry, there is a tender beckoning. The Beloved voice is drawing, whispering, inviting, welcoming, and when we step forward with genuine abandon, we find ourselves in the heady embrace of the One our soul does love. We are captured and sent deeper into Him. It is a beautiful falling.

THERE

At the end of last year while studying for a class series, I literally felt myself tap into something in God; somewhat like the nurse who is looking for a workable vein and finally hits it. In a very spiritually visceral sense, I believe that is what took place. I felt something surge in the Spirit when I touched on one simple point, that of hungering for *all* of God. I began to sense His voice speaking to my inner man and my pulse took flight, as I heard Him whisper through my Spirit... *Do you really want to go There?*

Yes, God, I automatically responded. But, in my mind, I was thinking, *Oh, no you didn't! You did not just go There!*

For, you see, between He and I, *There* has been painstakingly predetermined. We have been talking about *There* for quite some time now. It has been a topic of much conversation and the source of plenteous tears. He has known my desire to go *There*, for it is He who has placed that hunger inside of my heart. *There* has always been the central gravity point, the Bermuda Triangle of deeper spirituality. Some go *There* never to return, and those who do, well, it is their stories that fly under our Spirit radar and take out the defenses… the ones that protect us from deeper hungers and higher loves.

Let me whet your appetite and stir you just a bit about *There*. *There* is a place in Him that consumes the breath and refills the lungs with God-Life. *There* is an illusive Atlantis that one speaks of but cannot walk upon, an aroma wafting past the nose, never to be recaptured. *There* both frustrates and entices. *There* is a place of intense spiritual intimacy and heart-pounding challenge; a place of more than we dream possible, but have always somehow known exists. *There* is profound potential and deep grace, churning spiritual waters and personal revelation.

There is where He becomes all and we become less… and less is the most glorious of goals. I know, it makes no sense to the flesh, but oh, in the Spirit, it is a kid-in-the-candy-store kind of arrival. It's all *There*, everything God has to offer and I can scarce make a decision as to what I should taste first.

Oh, friend, I feel like He is taking me on the journey of a lifetime. I get this sense that I just cannot move fast enough. It is like searching for someone in a game of midnight flashlight tag. You know what you are looking for is just around the next tree, the next corner and your heart races at the thought of that uncharted encounter.

That is where I am at this point and time in my pursuit of *There,* my pursuit of Him. I know He is *There*…even though I have found Him here. I know He is calling. I feel an enormous sense of anticipation, a woeful groaning of Spirit laced with joyous pain-song, the highs and lows of searching with full expectation of finding and no timeframe of doing so.

God said when we seek Him with our whole hearts, He will be found. Ah and that, yes, that is the challenge, is it not; that *whole heart* business? For, we know with absolute certainty that all of our heart is not available. There is much heart-space offered to lesser gods and smaller pursuits, mundane and trivial holdings, trite servitude to thief lords, leaving us to seek Him with partial hearts, and find Him in part only.

And now, fellow travelers, we must determine if here is enough, or if *There* is truly worth the labor of un-dividing our hearts.

ETERNAL CONVERSATIONS

God is calling His children closer to Himself.

I know this, not because someone told me, but because I am experiencing it my own life. I used to think that God just wanted me to be good.

Now I know He just wants me close to Him.

Period.

The rest will take care of itself.

It would be great to be good enough to approach Him, but if we wait for that…well, it just isn't going to happen. I keep thinking, if I could work out the whole perfection thing we might get somewhere, but both He and I know that is not going to happen on this side of eternity. So, what we have covenanted to do in the interim is to stay as close to one another as possible.

From here to eternity, so to speak.

He is staying as close as is welcome.

I am staying as close as my disobedient flesh will allow.

I pray every day for more of Him and less of me, then stand amazed when a fiery trial comes along that burns away a tad of flesh. Indignant, I turn accusing eyes to Him. "What's going on here, God?" I ask in my most perplexed voice.

"You asked for more of Me and less of you…"

"Yeah, but you never said it would hurt!"

"Oh really? Have you heard of Peter?"

(I Peter 4:12 to be exact… Dear friends, do not be surprised at the painful trial you are suffering, as though something strange were happening to you.)

"Okay, but can't I have more of You without less of me? I mean, I can make lots of room for you."

"No, Child. You really are too full of yourself…"

"Ouch! That hurt!"

...do not be surprised

And the perfecting process goes on.

LEAVES

I once wrote a song entitled *"Seasons Change."* I was going through a change of seasons in my own life (I call it "changing seasons" because that sounds better than saying my life was falling apart). I had become very focused on the fact that I was no longer a child and became overwhelmed by my grown up responsibilities.

    I had two young children who thought I was actually supposed to know what I was doing, and a husband who had moved us six hours away from my family. The Gulf War was in full swing and I was living in a state of full-blown panic. My emotions took over and I became an unbelievably emotional mess. I really let Satan do a number on me (though I did know better) and by the time he was through, I felt like I was having a complete breakdown.

I think I actually longed for the oblivion of a breakdown...

I remember my husband coming home from work one evening and finding me crying in the bedroom. When he asked me what was wrong, I of course, could not put it into words, but he kept pushing. Finally it all came tumbling out something like this...

"I was watching and Saddam Hussein is going to blow everything up and there is a fault-line that runs across this area of the country and they predicted an earthquake, and Matthew is never going to have any hair because Aaron's teacher pinched his arm and the vacuum cleaner had smoke coming out of it and there's no money for anything, and the world must be coming to an end, because long-distance phone calls to my mom just make me miss her too much."

My poor husband looked at me for a moment, and with all of the compassion of a grizzly bear said,

"If you don't pull it together I'm sending you to your mother!"

What he failed to understand was that right then, I wanted nothing more than to be with my mother. He thought he was making a threat, I thought he was dangling a carrot in front of me. It makes me laugh now. It made me mad then.

I was losing it and he did not know how to handle me. The leaves were falling off my tree, a season of my life was fading away, and I did not know what to do. I had come face to face with the fact that I was an adult woman and had somehow found myself in the middle of a life I had not planned.

I needed help. I needed a spiritual mother, someone to lead me through a difficult time until I could have my feet firmly planted in that new season.

Times like this come for all of us. These are the times when we look around and see ourselves living what appears to be a stranger's life. We look up one day and find the landscape is alien and we are not sure how we got where we are or where we are headed next. These are times when we would love to be little girls again. We would love to have strong arms, wise words, and a comforting lap to crawl up into - someone to make sense of the confusion.

Well, my friend, we really do have just that. We have a Father who longs to take care of his little girl. He waits only for his child to ask.

Change is one of the few absolutes of life and beyond change lays the unknown. Only God can lead us through the changing seasons of our lives and into the beauty of our tomorrows.

He is a very loving Father…and He has a way of reminding us that, though we feel bald and barren, exposed and drafty, new leaves will appear with the next season and we will once again feel full, covered, glorious and secure.

Of late, I find myself with these words constantly upon my lips…

Please, Father…just a few more leaves.

BECOMING REAL

One of my favorite books of all-time is the Velveteen Rabbit by Margery Williams. We are probably all pretty familiar with the story. It is the story of a small toy rabbit, made of velveteen fabric, which is brought into a young boy's nursery. It has no particular gift and is immediately scared and intimidated by the "more gifted" mechanical toys. The rabbit meets the older, wiser Skin Horse –

"The Skin Horse had lived longer in the nursery than any of the others. He was so old that his brown coat was bald in patches and showed the seams underneath, and most of the hairs in his tail had been pulled out to string bead necklaces. He was

wise, for he had seen a long succession of mechanical toys arrive to boast and swagger, and by-and-by break their mainsprings and pass away, and he knew that they were only toys, and would never turn into anything else. For nursery magic is very strange and wonderful, and only those playthings that are old and wise and experienced like the Skin Horse understand all about it."

The Skin Horse begins to speak into the life of the Velveteen Rabbit and explains that love is the reason he looks so roughed up and well worn, but that love is the only thing that will ever make you completely real. My favorite passage from the book is this:

"What is REAL?" asked the Rabbit one day, when they were lying side by side near the nursery fender, before Nana came to tidy the room. "Does it mean having things that buzz inside you and a stick-out handle?" "Real isn't how you are made," said the Skin Horse. "It's a thing that happens to you. When a child loves you for a long, long time, not just to play with, but REALLY loves you, then you become Real." "Does it hurt?" asked the Rabbit." "Sometimes,"

said the Skin Horse, for he was always truthful. "When you are Real you don't mind being hurt." "Does it happen all at once, like being wound up," he asked, "or bit by bit?" "It doesn't happen all at once," said the Skin Horse. "You become. It takes a long time. That's why it doesn't happen often to people who break easily, or have sharp edges, or who have to be carefully kept. Generally, by the time you are Real, most of your hair has been loved off, and your eyes drop out and you get loose in your joints and very shabby. But these things don't matter at all, because once you are Real you can't be ugly, except to people who don't understand."

Oh, dear ones, just as the velveteen rabbit would become real only as it was really, really loved by the boy, *we only become real when we really, really, allow ourselves to be loved by God.* Or perhaps a more accurate way to put it is this... *we become more and more real every time we allow someone to see and love the real us.* Not the *us* we paint and powder, but the us that carries the very breath of God.

Do you understand how beautifully and perfectly you were created? Do you understand that

He thinks you are exceptional just as you are? One scripture says – *The King is enthralled with your beauty, honor Him for He is your Lord.*

I believe that when we become brave enough to get real, we honor Him. When we stop hiding and pretending and covering up, I think God just steps back and goes... *Ahhhh, there you are.*

My sweet friend, becoming real is about stepping out of the person everyone has convinced you that you are, and perhaps even what you have come to believe, and moving into who He is telling you that you were created to be.

Now, before anyone starts to panic, picturing yourself ducking behind racks in the mall before friends see you without makeup let me tell you that *real has nothing to do with the exterior,* but is absolutely completely internal. Being real is not about performing. It is not clothing or hairstyles or gifts. Real is not about anything on the outside, but everything on the inside.

You know, when the rabbit asks the Skin Horse if it hurts to be real, you can almost hear the shouts of thousands who have been wounded on the "real field"... *Yes!*

We all know the answer to that one. For, we all know that open hearts can sometimes become very tender targets. We put ourselves – our real selves — out there and run the risk of being rejected, wounded and hurt. But we risk the pain because being real, being authentic, and being fully loved, is worth it.

What the Lord has been teaching me of late is that fake gives birth to fake. Phony has baby phonies running around, and we have nothing real with which to work in His Kingdom. You see, fake is shallow. There's no substance to shallow. A mask is merely a thin veneer; there is no strength in it. But beloved, there is great strength in through and through real.

God desires real.

If you are perfect, how can you understand when I fall? If you have no flaws, then I am definitely going to keep mine hidden. But real? That is a different story.

You know you have a real friend when they can walk into your house and you are not worried about the cobwebs in the corner. You know you have touched a real place in relationship when the externals no longer enter your mind. A real friend actually has nothing to do with the external, but is the heart and spirit of one you love. Do you have friends like that? Friends that get in such a hurry to get to your child's school (since they are your emergency contact) that they actually show up in their house shoes? Your circles of friends…are they real?

We need people in our lives who will speak to the fake in us and say, "Oh, stop it! Who are you kidding?" Scripture tells us that "Faithful are the wounds of a friend." Is there someone in your life who will step in and risk it for Christ's sake? Oh, friend, we can lose sight of real if we live in fake-land too long.

You know, I was driving home the other day thinking about nothing in particular when I stuck in an Alison Krauss CD. I listened as she sang the verse to a song and I couldn't help it, I started to cry at one simple phrase… *There's always someone at home who never forgets who you are…*

I cried because there was a period in my life when I lost me. I had become everything everyone told me I was supposed to be, so much so, that I could no longer even remember what I was really like deep on the inside. When Alison sang, *always someone at home who never forgets who you are,* I immediately thought of my mother, and the innocent child I was when I was under her roof. Tears streamed down my face as I thought about how far I had come from the heart of that child. That child took great pleasure in having her picture taken with chicken pox and no front teeth. That child thought makeup was yucky and a hairbrush was best used on the cat. She thought dresses should be outlawed and high-heels were instruments of torture (that still holds true). That child thought fun was found in mud puddles and laughter was the most important thing in the world.

I cried because I missed her. I felt very detached from her somehow. Yes, I know that 42 years leave a mark, but the mark should not change us completely.

The Father had me do something that day when I arrived home. I pulled out all of my old photo albums and searched for pictures of me as a child. I even called my mom and asked her to send a couple of them that I remembered from her books. As I looked at these pictures, the Lord began to help me remember the heart of me. I had moved so far away from that place.

By the time I left the room that evening, I remembered. I remembered the things that were important to that girl then and should have been important still.

Playing lost in space with my little sister on our front porch; making mud pies with acorn topping; laughing until my sides ached.

I tucked one of the small black and white pictures into my wallet for forgetful moments; those moments when the fake me shows up to perform and pirouette. I simply pull it out and God speaks a million things to me without ever uttering a word.

Dear One, *His* creation is a million times greater than who you have created yourself to be… and who others have tried to shape you into. It is so cliché' but *Baby, there ain't nobody else in the world like you.* You are profoundly perfect in design and destiny. You cannot improve on what the Master has already done. It is like putting a velvet paint-by-number over a Picasso. Be who you are – a pure and holy child of God. Be free to show people the beauty God created.

I listened to an interview the other day and the woman on the screen said – "The greatest gift my family ever gave me was knowing who I am."

Does anybody really know you? Do you really know yourself?

Oh, my friend isn't it time for you to take off all the masks and let people see — and more importantly, for you become — who you have always been on the inside. What marvelous gifts we could give one another… an open heart, unguarded love, generosity and compassion. True gifts. God's gifts.

Oh yes, you shaped me first inside, then out; you formed me in my mother's womb. I thank you, High God—you're breathtaking! Body and soul, I am marvelously made! I worship in adoration—what a creation! You know me inside and out, you know every bone in my body; You know exactly how I was made, bit by bit, how I was sculpted from nothing into something. Like an open book, you watched me grow from conception to birth; all the stages of my life were spread out before you, The days of my life all prepared before I'd even lived one day.
Psalms 139:13-16 (Message)

I believe that today is one of those wondrous days He has recorded in that book. And what a marvelous thing if on that page the words were written... *Today, she becomes real.*

Becoming Real

Years spent trying to be
Everything everyone wanted from me
I'm just so tired of wearing the mask
Finally got desperate enough to ask

Can I be real?
Touchable breakable, bendable, real?
Can I be real, and not be afraid?

Tears fell, sad deep inside
Keeping my secrets while trying to hide
I'm too old to be living this way
I've made my decision, got something to say

Can I be real?
Touchable breakable, bendable, real?
Can I be real, and not be afraid?

Free now, a beautiful sight
There's peace in accepting I can't get it all right
From my heart of hearts a song does arise
Releasing one vision, it soars toward the skies

I will be real…
Touchable breakable, bendable, real.
I will be real and not be afraid.

AND ALL THE THREADBARE RABBITS SAID:

AMEN!

Stories from the Water's Edge

Thank you for joining me in the Mist.
May we journey again soon.

Still Mistified,
Barbie

www.ingramcontent.com/pod-product-compliance
Lightning Source LLC
Chambersburg PA
CBHW071927290426
44110CB00013B/1504